AF572127

Journey

A Collection of Essays

Adrienne G. Cannon

Bear Paw Press
7322 Range Rd,
Alexandria, VA 22306

Copyright ©2004 Adrienne G. Cannon

Library of Congress Catalog Number 2004105632

International Standard Book Number
ISBN 0-9748589-0-0

Valley Graphic Service
Frederick, Maryland
Printed in the United States of America

Dedication

To: Joel Robert Cannon
my husband and traveling companion in this journey

PREFACE

My first attempt at organizing a collection of my essays was so satisfying that I am doing it again! I have numerous people to thank for supporting me. Many of my friends and family have served as my "preferred reader's group" and have reflected back to me favorable comments.

My best friend Shelly Schwab, a fine writer herself, has given me much technical help as well as emotional support. My brother and sister-in-law, Julian and Donna Gokhale, spent many hours proofreading numerous drafts and have contributed innumerable helpful suggestions. My husband, Joel Robert Cannon, in addition to taking all of the photographs I have used to enhance my essays, took care of all of the publishing details that the "writer" part of me does not like to deal with. Friend and neighbor Lee Anderson, of Anderson Multimedia, freely gave his professional assistance to ready the digital photos for printing.

Mary Anna (Mimi) Grove, my editor, came into my life at just the right time, through the Washington Independent Writers group. She encouraged me in my efforts, cleaned up my punctuation, gave me helpful suggestions for rewording awkward phrases, and advised me on the ordering of this small volume.

I have not been alone in my "Journey." I send my most sincere thanks to all who have helped me in this effort.

Adrienne G. Cannon

September 2004

Photos taken by Joel Robert Cannon

Journey

Family and Friends

Past and Present

Family and Friends

Generations

My father, born to an Indian mother and father,
grew up in India under English rule.
He studied in English schools,
spoke with an English accent,
but roundly criticized the government
that controlled his life.

His father, a university professor,
fought with government officials
about his political philosophy.
They threatened dismissal, and so he, and his family,
migrated to America.

I was born here, married and had a son.
He studied English literature
and now lives in England teaching
courses on Chaucer and Shakespeare at a university.
His son, our grandson,
was born there in February.
He is English.

What would my father say to that?

Raymond Christopher Fleming,
great-grandson of Madhu S. Gokhale,
was born February 26, 2001

February 2001

Cambridge University, England

First Photo

Holding the envelope in my hand on a day shortly after your birth, I anticipate opening it and seeing you for the first time. I wonder if the photos inside will inspire me to sigh and coo and exclaim "Oh, how cute!" as I had always done when my friends showed me photos of their grandchildren.

I am alone this day, as I open my mail, and I will not have to assure anybody that you, with your diminutive face are, indeed, the most beautiful newborn in the world. These photos will show me your tiny features: your eyes, your nose, and mouth that will contain a little part of me. It is different, I thought, now that I am the grandmother. I know that you will be cute and adorable but what else will I see in that photo of you, my first grandchild?

I look into the envelope and extract a small pile of photos. I begin sorting through various shots but come to a quick halt with the view of a slight bundle, curled up in your mother's arms, your skin smooth, eyes tightly closed, hair still wet, your petite mouth, quiet for now, awaiting the next feeding. So you are the baby who will grow up and call me "Grandma." I pause in awe.

I study the other photos your father sent but keep returning to the same one that seems to have been taken in the first moments of your life. I have not seen you until now. I don't know who you are or what kind of a person you will be. I will tell my friends, when I speak to them about your photos, that you are "cute," perhaps the cutest baby I have ever seen. But that is not the word I am thinking of.

You captivate and enchant me. You are an intriguing stranger whom I want to get to know.

There have been many more photos since the first ones. You are growing and assuming an identity of your own. You look at the camera with bright and inquiring eyes; your hands are delicate, your feet always in motion. Your grandfather and I search for the parts of you that reflect us – the color of your hair and eyes, the shape of your nose, the size of your ears. You disappoint neither of us, taking on a different appearance in each photo as the months pass.

But I return time and again to your first photo and dwell on it. You are a beautiful creature as you make your appearance into the world you are to inhabit. Though linked to me, you are a new life that belongs to the next generation. I struggle to find the true word to describe you to my friends. There is none.

July 2001

Why?

Mommy!.....Mommy!..... Mommy!......don't leave me. Please don't leave me again! I need to be near you, feel your warmth, suck from your breasts, know that you love me. Why do you have to leave me all the time. Nobody ever comes to hold me. I lie waiting on my blanket staring at the crib bars. Sometimes I can see someone look in at me but I never say anything or even cry. I don't want anybody but you.

What happened to Daddy? It was nice when he was here. I liked it when we all ate together while you cuddled me. Then Daddy would play with me. He was rough but never hurt me. He is stronger than you and can catch me when he throws me in the air. You always screamed when he did that and told him to stop. But he and I just laughed at you and then rolled over together in a heap. Why don't we do that anymore?

You are so sad and tired. Where do you go everyday? It is so dark when you leave and I am sad, too, and lonely. I want to play in the sunlight and run in the rain, but you are not here to take me out. Once, I remember that you wrapped me against your body, and the three of us went for a walk. I could hear the birds and the sounds of other children playing. Can we do that again? Make Daddy come back so we can do that again.

The days are so plain and cold without you. I am trying to be good. I play with my fingers and toes. I like the flowers on my blanket and can stare at them forever. But sometimes I can't help crying because I miss you so much. I am hungry and shivering. I feel so alone. But you don't come to me. Why?

Today you hugged me especially tight and dressed me in a new sleeper suit. I hope we are going to find Daddy and be together again. I don't want you ever to leave me. I am afraid of anybody but you and think I will die inside if you leave me forever.

You are big and beautiful.....the words Daddy and I chose as your name when you were born. You were conceived from our love for one another. You came to make us a family, and we loved you so much from the moment we knew you would soon come into our world. We were so happy, the three of us. We would take walks together, eat together and talk and play in our own secure world.

My baby girl, it was so sad the day they told me Daddy was killed in the accident. I thought I too would die. But I knew I had to continue for you and for the memory of our little family. My work as a seamstress is so hard and takes so many hours! I can't bring home very much to you, but I have to work for our food and rent. The ladies in the building promised me they would look after you, but I know that you are alone too much.

I try to hug you and care for you when I am at home. But that is not very often. What do you do during the hours I am gone? You are so young. How can I tell you how much I love you and how I suffer during the hours we are separated?

They are going to make me leave next week because, as hard and long as I work, the money I earn is not enough to pay for our room any more. Oh, my beauty, I can't make enough money to feed you. Nobody will care for us because your Daddy is gone, and I can't make them understand that, even without a man living with us, we are still a family.

They told me there is a place where I can leave you, and somebody will come and get you. You are so young that maybe you'll forget about me and become someone else's big and beautiful girl.

Oh, how can I do this to you? How can I leave you, my love? What will I do when I don't have you to hug and kiss and feel your chubby body against mine? Can I survive without you? What will I do on your birthday without you at my side to remember that day? Will you remember me on that day? Will some other mother tell you that you are hers and give you gifts of love that are really from me?

Come. Here is a new, clean sleeper that they gave me in which to dress you. Let me hug you tightly. I love you. I will miss you. I will always think of you. Don't forget me. Please trust me, and when you see your new mother, see me inside your heart.

Tae Mi Cho was adopted by the Cannon family
when she was 18 months old.

September 1996

Middle Child

The night I was born there was racial disorder on the streets of Washington, DC. Not the big riots that followed the assassination of Martin Luther King Jr. Just some smaller disturbances that hardly caught anyone's attention. My entry into the world on a night that no one remembers seems appropriate. I don't mean to sound depressed about my life. It is just that I feel that I have to work very hard to make my presence felt.

I am the second child in the family, and for three years I was the little sister. My parents would fuss over me because I was petite and cute, and my big brother, who thought I was funny and helpless, protected me. I knew how to make my wishes known, and in those years, I usually got what I wanted.

Then my parents adopted a Korean infant who became <u>my</u> little sister, and I became the middle child. Suddenly I became almost invisible. All the neighbors came to see my exotic little sister, and my friends wanted to play with her, not me. My brother began to spend more time reading and writing. My parents were busy with their jobs and with all the babysitting arrangements needed for the three of us. Now I didn't get the things I wanted so easily anymore, and my requests were either denied or ignored.

I always loved to dress up, and when I went shopping with my mom, I asked her to buy me new outfits all the time. What arguments we had! When she gave in she always would look to see that I would wear what I bought. I really hated that. Sometimes I would not wear the new stuff just to make her mad – and to get her attention. I don't think she really noticed when I started to really care about the way I looked. She would just complain and worry about the money I spent on cosmetics, jewelry, and trendy clothing.

It was easier to get my dad to buy me things when we were out shopping. When he was involved in a serious discussion with my brother, I would ask him for anything I knew my mom would not let me have. It worked every time. He didn't even notice.

Sometimes I felt as if I were growing up all by myself and that I was the only one noticing the changes happening to me. One day, I looked in the mirror and the chubby, awkward person that I had always been (and indulged with French fries and sodas) had disappeared. I was looking at a tall, slender, young woman. There was a poise and confidence in that image that surprised me. Though I had felt this person developing inside of me, I never saw recognition of my growing maturity reflected in anyone's eyes. How could they not notice now?

I listened for my parents to brag about me and compliment me, but what I heard was more talk about my brother's accomplishments and my sister's development. I always got added into the conversation, but my news always seemed to be an afterthought.

I am close to thirty now. Since my college years, I have lived alone and held responsible jobs. I know that my business clients see me as skilled and confident, and that is important to me. But I know that in the eyes of my family, I am still the child whose news and needs come after the others.

A "business woman!" I had just heard myself say that when describing my daughter to a friend. I have watched her mature from a brash college senior into the confident, career-oriented, young woman she is today. When did my middle child become this poised, fashionable, and skilled person?

I remember the day she was born...or rather the night, because there was some rioting in the streets of the city. There was also a magnificent thunderstorm. The night was a beautiful entry into the world for a child I knew would make her presence known from that day on.

She was a difficult child because she had a strong will and was not shy about letting us know exactly what she wanted. Her dad, I, and her big brother knew that she was not just a cuddly little sister but a new force in our family circle. She didn't seem to miss a beat when we adopted a younger sister. Then, because she had to compete with another sibling, her strong will drove us to distraction. But we secretly admired her tenacity.

Trying to be a well-informed mother, I did lots of reading about child-rearing and about the middle child. It appears so easy in the books: special time for each child, monitor the competition between siblings, be fair, be kind, be...a perfect parent. Why is life never the same as it seems to be in the parenting books? So her dad and I probably overcompensated, indulging her developing personality as the most demanding sibling. Whether it was clothes, cosmetics, or jewelry, she usually got what she wanted.

What was she thinking about when she became the older sister, taking her place between our two other children? I could sense that on many days she felt depressed and ignored. I could never find the right words or actions that would convince her that she was important to us, just as important as her older brother and younger sister.

And now, the awkward teenager that she was, had been replaced by a beautiful young woman. I always knew that this spirited, over-indulged daughter, who loved to eat all her meals at quick food restaurants and who spent so much time fooling with cosmetics, would one day mature into the person she is today. Today her demanding nature has been translated into a person who can get things done, a person who doesn't accept anything less than the best.

She has been on her own for many years now, and it is hard to envision her as that small baby born on an angry and stormy night nearly thirty years ago. I am quick to tell everybody about my grown-up daughter. Could I ever convince her that she is the first one I talk about? Does a middle child ever believe that she sometimes comes first?

May 1997

Photo Albums

It's a nice room. I come here when I feel nostalgic. The albums are here, stacked against the wood paneling. The decorator told me that the room looks like a throwback to the 60's. How could she know how right she was, for that's when the albums start.

It is hard to believe my eyes when I look at the first one. There were just the two of us. I can barely remember how it feels to be a couple, just Bob and Adrienne. We planned our days around two schedules; we stayed out late and went to our jobs thinking only of the day's work. We came home to our loyal dog waiting patiently for his walks.

I do remember the dreams – children, a house, some challenging career, and we hoped we would earn enough money to travel. And yes, we would need to pay for the inevitable colleges that our hypothetical children would attend.

Look at the next album! There are our mothers just as we remember them. Vibrant and opinionated, both of them (and what a legacy they gave us). And look at our fathers, from opposite ends of the earth, India and California, both dashing, tall figures. Here are the pages when the photos of the children start. First, there is Chris with his bright, knowing eyes. Then there was Alyssa, an imp with an attitude even then. I remember that photo taken in the airport the day Tae arrived from Korea. She looked so little and lost in the arms of the flight attendant.

It is starting to blur. There are so many of them! Class photos, birthday parties, days at the beach. Soon come the graduations from high school and college. Look at this one. It is Tae's Jimmy at her graduation dinner ten years ago. And there is each of us with one or another of the children, or sometimes we are posing with a friend whose name is forgotten.

Time to move on. Let me look at the last few albums. The children are starting to drift away. I remember the summer we visited Chris and Juliet in England. And Alyssa and Michael gave us these photos of their visit to the beach and of a trip to Maine to visit his family. There are just a few photos of shy and modest Tae and Jimmy. It is good we have captured a few snap shots of them on big occasions.

Here is the last album. Funny. These photos are of just the two of us. There we are on safari in Kenya and in the Forbidden City of Beijing. We have made up for the shots of the missing children with many, many photos of our big, loveable Bear dog. I've got to show this last album to the kids when they are here for Christmas. No, I can't do that. I forgot for a moment. This is the first year that they will all be elsewhere on that day. Is that what they call an empty nest? Or are we again the couple who started the story told in these albums?

December 1998

For Just A Brief Moment

Your room, now a guest room, seems empty. It is not completely bare because your bed, with the red bedspread you chose, remains, as do some art prints, decorating the wall. There are a few knickknacks on the bookshelves and a book or two that you didn't want. The Korean dress you wore on your graduation day hangs alone in the closet as if waiting for you to claim it.

We encouraged you to take your belongings to your newly acquired condo. You resisted for a long time, and we wondered if you were delaying your move for a little while longer because you felt attached to your room where you grew up, in our house, a part of our family. Maybe, we thought to ourselves, you were reluctant to leave us.

From your first days with us we tried to imagine the transition you were making from your early days in Korea. You had been separated from your birth mother for more than a year, and just a day before we met you, you left your youthful playmates behind in the agency. We knew that for months you were not able to understand our words spoken in a language you had never heard before. We hoped you could sense our love and caring through our tones, looks, and hugs. We feared you would not easily overcome the trauma of being separated from your first mother, and you would be forever affected by the loneliness and neglect of the orphanage. You came into our world after an exhausting 24-hour flight on which you were tended to by strangers. They placed you into our arms, our anxious faces studying your tiny features.

As the months passed, it seemed that you adapted readily to all the new things surrounding you. We were charmed by you, the little sister of the family. You and your brother and sister were good friends most of the time though there were fights and rivalries. Some were deeper and longer lasting than we would have wished them to be. Oh yes, you had a temper, and though you were mostly quiet and accepting, there were the fiery outbursts. We did not always know what angered you, but we encouraged you to help us understand. We sensed your utter frustration at not being able to tell us what you were feeling and fearing.

The high school years, hard years for most teens, seemed the easiest for you. You joined the running and swim teams and shared a camaraderie with your teammates. When they encouraged you to keep up, even though you often came in at the end of the race, you would laugh with them and enjoy their attempts to inspire you. Schoolwork kept you busy, and though timid and quiet in your classes, you earned the compliments of your teachers who sensed your struggles with shyness.

When you asked to be permitted to attend a private school where the classes were smaller, we agreed. There was a small circle of friends, an occasional sleepover, and a lovely graduation dinner with a few of your closest companions. You wore your Korean dress, put on makeup, and smiled proudly at our pleasure when we told you how lovely you looked.

But there were always the dark days when you were so depressed you would stay in your room. Sometimes you would sleep for hours. Holidays were always the worst, and though we tried not to pressure you, we were sad when you could not bring yourself to join us in the festivities. At those times the scars of the past seemed to catch up with you, and rather than drawing closer to us, you retreated further and further away.

We tried to reach you, yet none of us, your parents, siblings, therapists, nor friends have been able to cross into your private world. Perhaps the memory of your early years, a time before we knew you or you knew us, is so heartbreaking you have buried those thoughts beyond recall, and they cannot emerge from that hidden place.

And now you are gone. It seems that you were with us for just a brief moment, a fleeting passage through our lives. You came to us from another world, filled with memories we cannot perceive. We peer into your room and think of your time with us, and we miss you. Will you come back to us when you have found the answers to the thoughts and feelings that elude you? We await your return to our caring family circle.

March 2002

Like Father, Like Son

The gardens and lawn that we see from the doorway of your office present a classic English backdrop. The stone buildings flanking the courtyard say "Cambridge" as clearly as any worded sign could. The setting strikes us as the perfect place to find you, tranquil and thoughtful while reading and writing.

Settled into this university town, you can pursue the same pleasures you loved while you were growing up. Your secluded office and the nearby libraries and reading rooms provide the solitude you need. Your office walls are lined with bookshelves filled with a collection of books used by you for research or read just for pleasure. Your name is on the binding of one of those books, others contain articles written by you, and shortly, there will be a second one bearing your name.

Since your youthful years, you have sought out scholarly locales and a few friends who could share your love of literature. When you went on to a university in New England, you found the niche you were searching for among the professors and students in your chosen field of English literature.

After graduation, we knew you would pursue an academic career, so your decision to accept a position at a major university in England, teaching and researching the works of Chaucer, was a happy choice. When we visited you there, we met your English colleagues, and you told us that there was one special friend together with whom you would establish a household. She too was a fellow at the university, teaching the works of Shakespeare and sharing your love of medieval English literature. Three years ago you and she had a son.

The first time we saw your son in your arms, he was sleeping peacefully, and it appeared that your nature and his would blend so well that your new parenthood would be effortless. You sent photos of him cuddled up in your lap as you read a book together. However, you had told us stories of how active he was in his mom's womb, and we wondered how long he would remain a placid, quiet baby.

As he passed his first and second birthdays, it became apparent to us all that, much as he likes his storybooks now clustered among your collection, he was developing a passion for noisy machinery. Lawn mowers, "diggers," steam rollers, bumper cars, and trains fascinate him, and your office is filled with brightly colored toys that make lots of noise – some can be pushed and pulled, some provide rides, and some can be used by a very young gardener. He also is full of ideas and opinions and most charming in expressing himself with clarity and insistence. We are amused at your struggle to keep up with the elemental exactness of his logic and his growing verbal expression.

He is a sociable boy and has many friends. This month you and his mom will celebrate his third birthday with a guest list that includes his nursery school classmates, their parents, and his teachers. The two of you, at one time used to a peaceful life in an academic setting, will find yourselves hosting a houseful of guests gathered to celebrate the day with you and to keep watch over the toddlers playing games, noisily chattering and singing, and eating, in their special way, birthday cake and ice cream.

We will think of you on this day and envision you, our son and our grandson, in the center of this happy scene. Over the years we have watched you blow out your birthday candles and mused about the person you would be. On this day of celebration of your son's birth, we think of you, our son, now a father. We join you in your wonder as to how much like a father is a son.

February 2004

Cambridge University, England

August 1st

The main avenue is just as it has always been, filled with summer visitors in all manner of vacation beachwear. The teenagers sport funky T-shirts and torn jeans cut off and fashioned into shorts, the parents and grandparents are more conservatively clad in coordinated tops and slacks, and the little ones wear almost nothing in the heat. We stroll along with the crowd, in our flip-flops or bare feet, dawdling in front of the shops.

Some of these shops date back to the beginning of the city's life, and some are brand new and sleek for this season; all are busy as soon as the first sleepy customers arrive looking for morning coffee and pastries. It seems to us that each year nobody has been here before to buy seashells, hermit crabs, sticky candy, painted tattoos, giddy photos, silver finger and toe rings, or beaded anklets, and all of these items need to be purchased again as quickly as possible. Maybe this will be the year we can win one of those stuffed animals for a dollar if ours is the first balloon to inflate. Or, maybe we will play skee ball on the boardwalk, a game that hasn't changed since our earliest visits to Playland.

Our ritual beach diet must be quenched: French fries, pizza, ice cream cones, and caramel crunch. Later in the day, fruit from the local farmers' stands will make up for the nutritional deficit, and there are some trendy nouvelle cuisine restaurants offering healthier food for our evening meal.

We walk onto the beach. The silky, soft sand waits for our well-worn towels and umbrellas, the same ones we use every year as a family tradition. We sit as close as possible to the surf line and as always, play a game with the tide. Even though we have an exact calculation as to the moment of the highest tide, we figure that we can outsmart the rhythm of the sea. So, it is just a question of time before we have to jump up and pull our towels, books, lotion, and water bottles back some inches just before they are inundated. It would not be a complete summer day if this rite were skipped.

When we were younger, we had no fear of the choppy waves of the North Atlantic and would wander into the wave line, bracing ourselves against the rough splashes and allow ourselves to be occasionally rolled over into the whitecaps. Now, with more experience, we calculate the timing between waves and can make it out to where swimming is possible. However, we still speak of the "big one" that "got" us and pounded us into the silt and broken shells. We admire the surfers' calm as they wait to ride the crest of the wave they chose and then let themselves gently fall into the shallow surf.

Our family's memory dates back over the more than 30 years we have come to this beach town on August 1st to celebrate our daughter's birth. We are in awe of the ocean and carry the image in our minds of the driving surf endlessly breaking over the sand, whether we are here, as today, or far away in our homes. We sense the waves that have been pounding onto this beach for millennia, and though we know differently, it seems that this small beach resort city has been here the same length of time. Though not a sentimental family, each of us who can fit the date on the calendar will come to the ocean for an annual reunion. It is, to us, one stable and secure place in a world that changes so quickly.

August 2000

The boardwalk
Rehoboth Beach, Delaware

Goodbye

".......Dal bastimento
verniciato di bianco
ho visto la mia città sparire,
lasciando
un poco
un abbraccio di lumi nell'aria torbida
sospesi"

G. Ungaretti, "Silenzio"

".......From the ship
painted white
I saw my city disappear
leaving
almost
a caress of lights in the silent air
suspended"

Pappa wrote the letter two months ago from America. He said that he is working as a carpenter now and has enough money for us to join him there. How far away it must be if it took such a long time for his letter to arrive. He must be very lonely. We haven't seen him for so long that I hardly remember what he looks like. We didn't want him to go, but he said that he should because there is no way to earn the money that we need here in our town. He wants me to go to the university, and if he returned, there would never be enough money.

I love my house and small room. I have to share it with my sister, and she is very mean to me. But I go out a lot with my little dog and play with my best friend. When I am tired of that, I read. The summer evenings are the best because there is light to read by for many hours. Will the sun shine into my room in America? Or will the buildings be too tall to let the light in?

The best times are when we eat together. I have too many sisters, and they are bossy. I wish I were not the youngest. Only when we eat at midday are they nice to me. I try to be good and not argue so much. My sisters can hardly stand new ideas. And they think that girls should be silent and agree with everything and everyone. When Pappa was here he would talk to me about his ideas and teach me how to say just what I wanted to say without getting my words all mixed-up.

When I walk to school with my friends we can see the seasons change. I am glad that we don't have to go to school after May because it gets too hot. Nothing will grow and the farmers get sad because there is not enough rain and everything dies. Many of them leave then and go to America. I wonder if they know Pappa. When it starts to cool off and winter comes we can run all the way to school in the morning and home in the evening. I hope I can still run to school in the city.

I buy the fruit for Mamma from the vendor. How do you get fruit in the big city? I love to pick the figs off the tree. Do they have fig trees in America? The baker, my friend, gives me fresh rolls when I come for the bread each day. I wonder if they have bakers in America and if the one I go to will talk to me.

How will I talk to him? He will speak only his language and I know only our language. Maybe there are bakers and fruit vendors that come from here who are living near Pappa now. And if I can only speak our language, how will I go to school? How will I read books? Will I be able to learn the language that they speak in America?

I see Mamma getting her suitcase, and I must get mine. What will I take from my house and room? I'll take my favorite book and the tiny rosary they gave me when I was baptized. I can't take Zuli. They don't allow dogs on ships. Maybe my friend will take care of him. I want to see her again to play our favorite games, but I am not sure I ever will.

Mamma said not to think about my house, my town, my dog, nor my friends. She is only thinking of Pappa and of where we will live in the city. She says that I will learn the new language and I will go to the university in America. Once the ship we are taking leaves the land and I see my town and country disappear, Mamma says that I should not look back.

Mamma, how can you forget our life here? I will try to think only of the future, but I think that I will always have a picture in my memory of this time.

Libera Rutigliano, my mother,
arrived in New York City from southern Italy in 1920.

December 1996

Ever Free

Ah, fors' è lui che l'anima	*Could it be he who stirred my heart,*
Solinga nè tumulti.....	*Lonely in life's confusion.....*
A quell'amor, ch'è palpito	*I have never known such love*
Dell'universo intero *Misterioso, altero* *Croce e delizia,* *delizia al cor.....*	*In the whole universe* *Mysterious and powerful* *Pain and delight, in my heart.....*
Sempre libera degg'io *Folleggiare di gioia* *in gioia.....*	*Let me be ever free* *to live for joy and pleasure only.....*

"Sempre libera," La Traviata

My father came to meet us at the dock. He looked different from what I remembered when we last saw him four years ago. His hair was sprinkled with gray, and his face looked a little older. He had a lift in his step that I had never seen before.

He and I resumed our talks that we had begun when I was very little. At all of our meals he would tell us about his political life, and I would question why he was so active supporting a political party that was so tiny. He explained to me how he felt about a person's right to be free mentally and physically. He reminded me how he had made my mother so angry when he named me "Freedom" and refused to have me baptized. I questioned him closely about all of his ideas. Sometimes our discussions became very loud, and my sisters and mother would yell even louder to try to quiet us.

But I loved the noise and exchange of ideas. With my father's encouragement I learned how to think critically about social issues that could change the way of life for all of my newly arrived friends and family and, really, for all people. He never showed disrespect for me because I was a girl. I teased my sisters because they never argued with anybody except among themselves. They really tormented me and called me a "libertarian and suffragette."

When I was accepted by the local college, he and my mother were happy that I would be the first in the family to continue with higher education. My mother would have preferred that I follow tradition and stay at home and marry a boy from my country, maybe even from my little town. My father saw, in my desire to continue my education, that I was truly his daughter and would pursue his ideals of freedom.

Did I love to argue! I joined every club on campus that would have me and loved the long evenings spent in argumentative discussion. Of course I was also looking to see which of the men who argued with me was also handsome and well-dressed. My father teased me because he knew that my interest in all the men I told him about was not strictly intellectual. And he could tell that I was a bit lonely because of my strong personality and desire to preserve my personal freedom, the very freedom he had taught me to cherish.

One night, instead of going to a meeting of a political club, I agreed to sing some operatic selections with my hometown friends at a recital. I was startled when one face in the crowd caught my attention. He looked out of place surrounded by all those young, almost identically dressed, student types. Instinctively I liked his demeanor. He was dark and tall and carried himself proudly. He wore a suit, as did the others, but he looked more formal, somehow more distinguished.

When he spoke, he had a British accent. But he wasn't British. In fact, he became incensed when I inquired if he were. He told me very directly that he was in America because of his dislike of what the British had done to his country's freedoms. It was immediately clear to me that this man was not shy nor was he without opinions. I remember that evening well! The discussions that we had were as noisy and as controversial as any I had had with my father.

He liked my name and my spirit. I liked his rhetorical way of arguing, though I got the best of him with every point. He had some old-fashioned ideas, but I excused him because he was struggling with his own upbringing that was very traditional. There was a part of him that was a mystery to me and that intrigued me.

I told my family about my new friend. "Friend?" said my sisters and mother. They knew there was more than friendship involved, and they did not like the fact that he was not from our country. My father smiled broadly and asked about his opinions concerning social justice and human rights. "This man is not easy to explain," I said. " He comes from a culture that has a religion that teaches acceptance of everybody but in practice freedom is restricted in many ways."

"Your name is Freedom," replied my father. "You must not allow anybody to take the joy and pleasure of being free from you."

How strong my father was, never to relinquish his feelings about the value of personal freedom! Could I resolve the confusion I felt and give up some of my freedom to live with this mysterious but compelling man? I trembled with indecision, but I began preparing my arguments with him for the future.

My mother, Libera Rutigliano,
married my father, Madhu S. Gokhale, in 1929.
They were married for more than 50 years.

December 1996

The Cheery Twin

It's the simple things that make her happy: a Barry Manilow CD, statues of pink flamingos in her garden, a favorite radio talk show. She leads a quiet life, happy to be home among her photographs, sitting in her favorite chair while she reflects on her day. She is widowed now and her days are solitary, but still she does not complain. A conversational phone call or occasional luncheon date pleases her and keeps her in touch with others.

She shared her room easily with her twin brother, letting him have his way so as not to provoke his anger. He had a brooding nature but would fuss and bluster when irritated. If she missed the attention her intellectually inclined family bestowed on her older sister's high academic grades, she did not outwardly show it. Her twin hid his defeats from view, harboring deep inside a darkness that nobody saw.

While growing up, she admired her older sister's academic discipline and tried to imitate her. But she was more content to play with dolls and imagined her future life as wife and mother. Her family was conservative and staid. So she waited until she was free from the family household restrictions to indulge herself in face makeup and fashionable clothing, both with a flair, though not outlandish.

Dating men who were unknown to the family was not approved of by her parents, and so she lived with the anxiety of knowing that she would have to wait until a proper match could be arranged. When she finally met the man who would become her husband, she was delighted with the choice, even though she did not initiate it. And with the birth of her son, her life plan was fulfilled.

She shared the same time and space in the family with her twin brother. But while she accepted her disappointments and eventually forgot them, his boiled below the surface. When he was discouraged by his parents from following his love of plants and flowers as a career path, he stormed and struggled silently. His torment never left him, and one day, tired of the strain and helpless to express his anger and frustration, he took his own life.

Twins. One lively and joyful, one somber and vulnerable. She, satisfied with her life and enriched by her son's successes, shares her good humor easily. Her twin brother is but a poignant memory. Her friends and family wonder at the curious destiny that separated the twin siblings in personality and outlook and chose her to be the cheery twin.

August 2002

Spy Story

Why had he not been more careful? His habit of arriving late had always been a source of arguments, but he had really pushed the limit this last time. It had been a good cover. She knew he liked to take his time in museums, so splitting up for a couple of hours was a good plan. She was happy to walk with her mother and father over to the Rue de la Paix to shop, and he could browse at his own pace. The time and place he had arranged with his contact coincided perfectly with her plans to drop him off at the Louvre. He had not foreseen any problems with the rendezvous.

He was an unlikely candidate for the job he held. His native knowledge of French had always been an extra advantage to him. But his world did not extend beyond his small town on the U.S. border with Canada. His parents were owners of a grocery store, and though his father read the paper everyday and his Mum (when he spoke of her he still used his childhood word for her) watched TV to catch the local news, their dinner table discussions were rarely about politics or news events. His brother preferred to talk about sports though he always had his head in a science book. They were good buddies, and their favorite times were spent together in the small hut they built on the lake so they could fish through an icy hole.

Both of them went to the local state university. He was never as serious about his studies as his brother, so it didn't surprise him when his brother got a scholarship to med school. When he was left alone at home, he got restless. Where to go to move on with his life? He had heard about a degree in international studies at a university in Washington, DC. Being already bilingual was a plus; he probably could get into the program easily. After a weekend visit, he found that, though the capital was a big city, on campus there was a small-town feel. And there were opportunities for comfortable, solid jobs if he followed a programmed course of study.

Hardly had he enrolled when a person whom he later learned was an "agent" contacted him. The proposal sounded innocent enough: he would get financial assistance for most of the program and, after getting his degree, he would accept a job with the State Department. The beginning salary was attractive as were the benefits. There were some briefing sessions he would have to attend so he could be prepared for his assignment. He did not know what they meant by "assignment," but they assured him that the briefings would prepare him with in-depth information about the country to which he would be assigned. Yes, it was a country with deep political rifts, but his job would be confined to analyzing written sources. Getting paid to read seemed ideal.

At first it was simple. He took local transportation to work (he never had to deal with big city traffic congestion), happily read the newspapers searching for news about "his" country, and then got to read internal memos that interpreted what the national reporters had written. He noticed that slowly the information he read got more ominous. The misery of the people halfway around the world whom he was reading about began to touch him and make him sad and uncomfortable. He was beginning to sense an urgency, a desire to go and see what was really happening.

So when they approached him about spending three months in the battle zone, he was anxious to go. Would he meet with the locals and give them some information? Of course he would. He would begin to learn their language now. He was a quick study, and until he was fluent, his French would probably work with most of his contacts.

When he arrived, it was cold but not unlike his hometown in January and February. His daily routine was the same as back in Washington, but he was surrounded by the devastation of a civil war. He and his co-workers helped out whomever they could. He grew fond of his language teacher. She was kind and gentle, a professional teacher, but her living conditions were miserable. When he went for his lessons in her house, he could hardly bear to see her in her poorly heated house and accept her generous offer of tea and biscuits from her bare cupboard.

One day she asked him to carry a message to the office. It seemed to be a simple favor. When her requests continued, he realized that he wasn't really aware of all of the contents in the envelopes she was giving him. And, after each delivery, the quality of the secret information that his office was collecting seemed better than ever.

The time came to go home. Slowly he was beginning to understand. From his first contact on campus, he was being groomed for a job that would require him to carry information. Now he was to monitor what was given to him to see that it reached the highest source in Washington. Once back at his desk, his new duties would include arranging contacts with other agents to obtain information that he would pass on. He had no choice. He, himself, was now an intelligence "agent," a spy.

Life seemed to return to normal at home. His girlfriend welcomed him without noticing any difference. It was easy to meet with his contacts outside of the office. He went to the gym regularly, and he could almost always arrange to meet in the sauna where there was privacy. If that were not possible, he could exchange materials by placing his gym bag next to his friend's for a drop. Sometimes he would take longer than promised, and his girlfriend would be really angry with him. But she had learned to accept his lateness as absent-mindedness. When she got over her pique with him, she would tease him about his small-town slowness.

He had already been asked to make another trip to that poor, devastated land he left the year before. When he told them that shortly he would be in Paris with his girlfriend and her family, they asked if he would meet with a contact there. The meeting place would be a cultural site that he was sure the family would visit. Meeting in the washrooms would be okay, but if he could arrange to meet alone, perhaps on a couch in front of a painting or in a small gallery, that would be better.

The wait was too long. He would have to leave or risk a scene with his girlfriend because he was once again late. Something must be wrong. He would call the number they gave him. Just then he was approached by the museum guard who asked him to follow him down the hall. There he saw her sitting on a bench.

His language teacher had flown in from her country with a special pouch for him. They embraced, happy to be reunited. She explained that she had trouble getting to the museum unseen and apologized for her late arrival. Things were better for her now that she had a secret source of income, but she had to be very careful. They spoke a little about conditions in her town, about the way the hostilities were going, but hastily concluded their conversation. He was reluctant to part so quickly, but he knew they would meet the following month when he again would visit her country.

Now he had to run to meet his girlfriend. She was gone! How could he explain to her what had delayed him? He couldn't tell her he was a spy. He would just have to endure her ire and pretend that he lost track of time. That would be his story.

February 1999

Summer Sisters

The final days of summer were approaching. Still, none of the four had made the phone call to set up their annual luncheon get-together. Looking at the calendar to check the dates of the last week of vacation before the local schools and colleges resumed classes, Alana called the friend to whom she felt closest. She was met with indifference and reluctance to commit to a date and time for the occasion.

What was wrong this year? Throughout their children's school years the summer luncheon was always a joyous time of sharing news about the past year and optimistic views of the coming year. Ever so often one of them would confess frustration about one or another of their children's development. And, in a kindly way, each of the friends would try to impart comforting and cheering words.

Eve was so proud of her daughter, an attractive and intelligent girl who came from Korea. She pleased her mother so often, while in elementary and middle school, with her artwork, her high scholastic grades, and her pleasing personality. Now in college, she seemed a bit directionless and Eve complained that her daughter's boyfriend was leading her astray. The past summer she had announced plans to travel with him across the country and live on the West Coast.

All of the friends were anxious to hear about Gloria's son who was planning to go to law school. Gloria had worked so hard during his childhood years to encourage him to exercise for his health and meet people, especially girls. He had overcome his extreme shyness, and by losing significant amounts of weight, had learned to socialize comfortably with his classmates at college. She was so devoted to her only child that her friends, with multiple children, had to remind her gently that she should give her son some freedom to develop on his own.

Tia's daughter struggled with being overweight as well and the past summer had gone to a camp especially designed to help teens lose weight. All of the women in her family struggled with extra pounds, so Tia could understand her daughter's struggle. But, nevertheless, the three friends could see her distress. They tried to get her to focus on her daughter's strong points and to be less obsessive with the weight issue.

Alana struggled with her own daughter's aloofness from the family. Her daughter, also Korean, and a promising writer in her high school years, had become angry and confrontational lately. Communication between mother and daughter was becoming nonexistent. Eve spoke to Alana as feelingly as she could about adopted children and their lack of trust. Gloria and Tia voiced their concerns with their children's sense of being different and comforted Alana with small anecdotes of success experienced by their own children.

As Alana spoke to each of her friends and pondered aloud this year's strange reluctance to set up lunch, Eve was the first to speak to her frankly. She just could not bear to hear the other women brag about their children's successes when her own daughter was floundering. Gloria conceded that, since she had filled out her son's application to law school, she could not discuss his plans without confessing what she had done. And Tia acknowledged that she just could not face her friends and their triumphant stories when her own daughter was, once again, obese.

Alana was secretly relieved. She would not have to tell anyone that her own daughter had moved away over the last year and had not spoken to her for months. She and her friends, who had been linked like sisters by the lives of their families, had gradually grown apart. Now their summer lunches would be suspended indefinitely. She was saddened and, as she reflected on the past summers, felt nostalgia for a time in their lives that had passed.

June 2001

Dining Out With Friends

Saturday night, we agreed,
would be perfect for a dinner date;
a foursome of close friends,
a fine restaurant, good conversation,
an evening to anticipate.

The maitre d', a pleasant man,
full of welcoming phrases and smiles,
led us not very far,
but, in just a bit of a hurry,
to a booth near the bar.

"There's smoke in the air,
said my friend, and sneezed,
while stating, "This isn't fair!"
"I'm allergic.....and gasped
as if she were seized.

"And the music is too loud!"
said her husband.
not at all too proud
to clamp his hands to his ears
to dampen the sound.

Mine, clearly too hot,
took off his coat and tie,
unbuttoned his collar,
and exclaimed, he "would die
of the heat."

As I squeezed my long legs
into that tiny booth,
I sighed and resigned myself
to the truth.........
about that evening just past.

Our date with four friends
was doomed from the start
and as soon as we ate,
we paid the bill
and made haste to depart.

"Another time and
we won't complain,"
we agreed, and said good night
while we crossed our fingers
behind our back with all of our might.

May 2003

Solstice Sisters

She was born, deep into December, far to the north where the cold winter nights never end and the summer days last forever.

I was born, in mid-June, in a temperate zone where the days are mild and the sun rises and sets to match the workday.

She was a city child and could hear the traffic from her room, walk to the shops, visit the great museum on the weekends, and play with her friends in the park near her home.

I lived in a house with a garden and sidewalks. I could ride my bike, roller skate, and play ball in front of my house. Once in a while my mother would take me on the bus and subway into the big city to shop and eat at the automat.

One day, the war came to her city, and she was sent to the country where there was food and her grandmother could care for her. Her parents did not see her often, and she worried that her father would be killed in the siege. Her grandmother was busy in the small wooden house and she played by herself while she thought about her city home and her mother and father.

I never knew hardship during the war years though I heard talk about a bomb that could kill all the people in a city in a flash. We saved string and aluminum and ate up all of our food because other people were starving.

After the war, she came back to the city, continued her studies and got her degree in foreign language education. She married a young student and had a son. She worked throughout his childhood and fretted that she could not give him all the attention and advantages that she wanted.

I went to the university in the big city and got my degree in foreign language education and married a young student. I had a son and was torn between commitment to my profession and a desire to be a good and attentive mother.

She came to my country to the school where I was teaching. I heard about a reception for the teacher that had come on an exchange program. She was there, hesitant, though seemingly poised. I went there wondering what she could be like. Could she share, in any way, my experiences, my life?

We spoke a little, and at once sensed that, though separated by an ocean, bureaucracies, and languages, we share a sisterhood. Now that we have found each other, we exchange our daily thoughts silently, and as the sun rises each day, we are linked. We are solstice sisters.

November 1996

Four Russian Women

Marina

She was born just as the last century began and was given the name of a saint. Her mother and father lived in the capital city and though the weather was often harsh, they stayed warm and fed in their small, humble flat. She went to school each day, and when she came home she would join her mother in the kitchen to sit in front of the fire with her cat curled up in her lap. She would read quietly while waiting for her father to return from teaching his classes at the agriculture college.

She especially loved poetry and began very early to write short, simple verses. On Sundays, they went to the local church and lit candles to the saint for which she was named. In the summer, she dreamed of the countryside, of the open air, and gardens full of flowers.

Almost from the beginning of her understanding she could sense a nervousness in the air. Her neighbors talked in angry voices, lamenting their difficult lives, and she heard critical words that blamed the ruler of her country and his friends for the poor conditions in which they lived.

Sometimes there were noisy parades in the streets, and one day she was told that her country was fighting a war with foreigners. While in her teens, she learned that the aristocratic ruler had been overthrown and a new life was starting for her country. Sadly, she learned that her church had been closed down. When her daughter was born, she could not take her to be baptized.

Elyena

At the time of her birth, her mother and father had accepted the revolutionary form of government and called her by a secular, yet lyrical name. She would live in the same flat in which her mother was raised. Women were considered equal to men by the new government, and she could go to the large university that was a short bus trip away. She loved flowers and growing things, as did her mother and father, and studied botany and biology. When she finished her studies, she accepted a job as a state biologist. Her husband used his degree to secure a prime job as military architect.

She traveled to work every day on public transportation and worked long hours. On the weekends, she and the family would escape to a modest country house they had built in a forest just outside of the city limits. Her mother would help with the housework, and when her daughter was born, the three generations formed a warm, loving circle.

Though she accepted the philosophy of the new regime, she never forgot her mother's devotion to the church, and the family secretly lit candles in their comfortable kitchen to celebrate the births and deaths of their friends and family. They loved to go to the theater and see the distinguished ballet, opera, and theatrical companies sponsored by the government. The tickets were a reasonable price for even the most humble citizen.

Ekaterina

After years of political strife in her country and a psychological war with the rest of the countries of the world, the year she was born brought a major confrontation with another world power. Her parents, mindful of the strong traditions of their country, named her after an empress who personified the greatness of Russia's past.

It was expected that she, like her mother, would study at the university, and since she loved to read and write, she continued on with her studies until she had an advanced degree. She got a job in an important government office as a political researcher. Lingering a little at the university, she enjoyed the academic life and the extra attentions of a young, attractive professor. She married him and began her family.

Her country was becoming more prosperous and more open to the rest of the world. She decided that her dacha in the country must have running water and electricity. She and her husband thought about traveling, even to the country that had shunned hers and made her countrymen seem unwelcomed. One year she did take that trip and discovered how much she loved the fashion, food, music, and opportunities that suddenly became available to her. She felt free and was glad that her country was also working to liberate itself from its past. She was pleased to discover that she, the first in her family, would have a second child, and later a third.

Mikhaila

Last summer, just two years after the new millennium began, she became the welcomed third child into her affluent and westernized family. She carries her grandfather's name, and it has a musical lilt. She came home, in her parents' arms, to her family's newly built condo, safe and secure in a gated community.

From her parents' room, where she sleeps in her cradle, she can see the magnificent building that speaks of another era and symbolizes, by its rigid tower, the restrictions of the past. But when her mother or nanny stroll with her outside, even on the coldest winter days, she can see the bright lights of her new world, of the local shops full of gourmet merchandise, the latest CDs, and videos and restaurants that feature food from around the world.

Her family still visits her grandmother in the family-owned apartment. She can feel that, though her mother's old home is simple, it represents the family's unity and won't be given up easily. But she is glad to return to her modern condo and already follows the moving figures on the giant TV, the colorful graphics on the powerful computer on the desk, and the rotating dish in the microwave. She responds to the musical jingle of the cell phone when her older sister calls from many miles away.

She senses that she will study at the university as does her sister and as her brother will too. She hardly perceives that she will speak not just her native tongue, but another language that she has already heard from friends and on the satellite TV channels. Healthy and happy, she enjoys her baby massages, the soothing sounds of classical music played by her mother, and the special gifts brought to her by her father from his travels around the world.

Although her young mind cannot yet consciously focus on her future, deep inside her is buried the memory of her family and the women, strong and vital, who will be her models for the future.

November 2002

Past and Present

Transformation

I don't understand how it can be that two people reside in my body.
The first, a perpetually busy achiever, seems less and less a
part of me.
The second, who takes hold of me more and more each day, is
energetic but has no drive to accomplish noble goals.

I am being transformed.

The change began when I stopped going to work
every day.

Retirement.

The years of checking in promptly and regularly ended.

Forever.

I ask myself if maybe I really didn't like my job.
Not true.
I was committed, convinced that each day in the classroom
contributed to the ultimate goal of a better world.
I joined committees, attended conferences, gave workshops, wrote
guidelines, and trained student teachers.

No effort was too much.

But I wearied of the years of routine.
Who doesn't get tired of going to work each day?

When the overwhelming number of students
and tasks got to be a burden, I thought I would rest and then teach again.

But no.

The person I am today cannot understand how the other taught
so many classes, guided so many students and made so many lesson plans.
Each day was framed by the classroom bell ringing
relentlessly.

Better world or no, I can't go back to that frenzy again.

Sometimes I get up early so that I don't miss the
morning hours when everything is fresh and the new day begins.
The house is pleasant with many windows, so I can
see the trees and flowers.

The birds, squirrels, and even deer come and feed,
and Bear, the dog, watches them with amusement.
The sun shines straight into my eyes
and then is gone in an early sunset.

Will I tire of this life?

Maybe one day I'll want a job again but for now,
I am learning to live with this new person
that has come to visit my body.

I hope she will stay.

December 1996

An English garden,
outside of London

Identity

I came to the Kennedy Center from my previous life where my identity was established and clearly delineated. I went to work each day and talked shop with my colleagues. Over the years I defined myself by the daily news I shared each day about my health, my family, and important moments in my personal history.

Then came retirement, and suddenly, the easy days that I anticipated for so long became a reality. There was no need to follow a demanding schedule, to fight the commuter traffic, or to squeeze in errands before and after the workday. Everyday became a Saturday or Sunday.

But something was missing. I could not exist just puttering around the house, reading the paper endlessly, and drinking innumerable cups of coffee. Even the long postponed projects didn't seem appealing if there was nobody with whom I could discuss them. The companionship of friends who could share what was going on in my life was missing. And I needed a schedule that meant that my presence was vital and that my skills would be appreciated.

The Kennedy Center attracted me because of the intellectual and aesthetic pleasures I knew could be found there. So I followed a training course that honed the skills I brought from my working career and found I could apply them to my new assignments. I began to look over my wardrobe critically and found a new incentive to dress up.

I began commuting again, but now it was my choice, and I rarely have had to cope with rush hour. My picture was taken, and I was given a Kennedy Center ID card to wear. Now when I report to my shift, ready to meet my newfound friends, I proudly don my ID tag and relish the sense that once more I have an identity.

February 2000

Rhythms

I remember the dreams that drifted through my mind during my working years. My commitments and assignments were relentless, and I visualized getting them all under control, completed, and put aside. Then I could sleep late into the morning, read for hours, sit in the garden with the dog, or stroll aimlessly in the shopping malls and drink lattés until I felt like coming home.

When retirement came, there were the months of euphoria when each day began with no plan beyond breakfast. Slowly my calendar filled up with pleasurable dates: lunches, swimming, dance class, and a few volunteer ventures. I started to set aside certain days so I would be a responsible volunteer, present on a regular basis. Yes, I said to myself, I need the regularity of knowing that I have a schedule, if only a minimal one, and that my presence is expected and my talents needed. How enjoyable it was to go to my weekly "job" for four hours.

The once-a-week engagements became a variety of jobs, and the limited schedule became a daily one. Without noticing, I had smoothly taken on band rehearsals and serving in theater coffee lounges in the evenings. Now, though I was home during the day, at least occasionally, almost all of my evenings were accounted for.

I had always prided myself on managing many activities at once. And I sought out and accepted all of the volunteer assignments willingly and enjoyed each one during the short duration in which I had to direct my attention to the task. Some days I wished I didn't have to get up so early and take the newspaper with me instead of lingering over it with my morning coffee. And now, sometimes, I had conflicts on certain dates and had to rearrange arrival times or skip one favorite thing for another. Arriving from my daily stint in the late afternoon and having to go out again for an evening activity, when was I to prepare and eat dinner?

Something had happened to the gentle rhythm of my retirement days. “You have every minute planned,” said a friend, intending to give me a positive message about my productivity but bringing into focus the pace of my undertakings. I had begun my old habit of making lists, so I could juggle commitments efficiently, and I recognized the familiar feeling of subtle panic that I would certainly miss an important event or deadline.

I was determined to manage this growing predicament. I know that the yearly calendar has a rhythm of its own. Fall is busy for teaching events with the opera and symphony and the Christmas season is always relentless with festive parties added into the schedule of other dates. Summer would be a good time to start letting go. My new resolution would be to, once again, savor the pleasures of getting a slow start in the morning and contemplate my free time.

Epilogue

I am restless now at the end of the summer. Quiet, sedentary endeavors don’t appeal. I think I’ll check my e-mail. Or I could practice for an upcoming concert. I need to study the libretto for next year’s operas. Perhaps this is a good time to write an article for the volunteer newsletter. Smoothly and imperceptibly I can feel the pace of my life accelerating once again. Maybe this time I can find the tempo that suits me...the rhythm of my life.

August 2000

Wondering

We aren't hippies, or boomers, or yuppies, or Generation Xer's. Is there a name for us? We were born in the late thirties and early forties, just as our parents were recovering from the depression. We can't claim to have grown up walking miles in the snow to school, doing homework by candlelight, or being astounded when man first flew, but our lifetime spans slow but steady changes that make our childhood look somewhat quaint, though not unpleasant.

The desks in our schoolrooms were bolted down and we sat in rows except for our reading circles. We wrote our high school papers by hand in a penmanship that was passable but never resembled the perfect script of our grandmothers. We typed our first college work on mechanical typewriters and finished graduate school using an electric typewriter if we could find one.

We figured our math on paper, and the most accomplished of us used a slide rule when we learned what to do with it. Eventually some of us had calculators and could finally escape the frustration of never being able to memorize those multiplication tables.

We used lead pencils ("#2 lead" hardly meant anything to us as our tests were scored one at a time by real people) and sharpened them with a crank sharpener. Occasionally, we used a Scripto mechanical pencil until the lead ran out, and we couldn't find any more.

At home we dialed the black telephone on a rotary dial, or perhaps some of us remember talking to an operator who asked us "Number, please?" The telephone had a special ring for each household, and if we were clever, we could lift the receiver silently and listen in on the party line. We had to sit down by the single household phone and could only move around to the extent that the short phone cord permitted.

Our household chores were not hard, but we did have to help wash and wipe the dishes. And when we were done with our dinner cleanup and had finished our homework, we turned to the radio each evening for our favorite drama programs. We still remember the awe with which our family received its first TV set into the living room (there were no rec rooms quite yet).

We played outside after school, and our roller skates had two wheels in front and two in back. There were no leather boots and these metal skates stayed on the front of our feet by means of a metal clamp that we tried to tighten, often uselessly, with a skate key. The wheels wore down on the cement streets if we skated with too much enthusiasm. Our bikes had no gears, and we had to backpedal to brake. We didn't wear helmets.

Those born after us will reminisce, in their golden years, about how much their lives have changed. They will cite the technological revolution to impress on their grandchildren that life is not "what it used to be." But will we, whose lives span the last 60 years, be able to properly convey to our grandchildren the quiet transitions that amaze us? I wonder.

July 2000

They Do Remember!

June. The last day. The last bell has rung. I see only their backs as they dash out of the room for the last time. The room empties quickly of their active young bodies. Left behind is the disarray of desks, scraps of paper, and a forgotten pencil.

On the walls are a few remaining posters and colorful prints left up so that I am not alone and facing bare walls. I take a moment to sit and think of the last few days. There were the usual "lasts" – the last lesson, the last test, the last attendance call. The books were turned in and the papers returned, grades were given, and fines paid. A few students gave me a card or a small gift, but none of them turned around to say goodbye before they left. They are young and live for the future. Am I alone among them in my reflections of what we had done together over the past year?

"Mrs. Cannon, Mrs. Cannon!" I hear the voice calling my name and know when I turn I will see a face that I know. The countenance will have matured, the body will carry a few more pounds. Someone has spotted me on the street and recognized me as their Spanish or Italian teacher of a past year. They greet me, smiling, and recall some memory from our classes together. Sometimes it is a long-forgotten classroom "food" day or the slides that I brought to them from Italy and Spain to entice them into traveling. Some of them traveled with me and remember eating rabbit or pumpkin flowers. Or, they speak of the contemporary Spanish singers we listened to or the Italian opera videos we watched together.

Many of my former students greet me at the Kennedy Center where we have both been drawn by our interest in music. An attorney in the audience, a young actress on her way to an audition, a financial officer who keeps the books for the Center, a National Symphony Orchestra Fellow on her way to a master class, a member of the opera chorus in rehearsal...each has a story for me, and a verbal or physical hug.

My students and I wearied of the daily grind when we were in the classroom day after day. But, together we built a store of rich moments that now we can recall as we contemplate our lives. I am not alone in my memories.

October 1998

Full Circle

As I entered the classroom of a Virginia high school, the class looked at me, expectant, hesitant, and waiting to learn the difficult and elusive foreign language I was to teach them. I was young and had very little experience teaching and those eager faces unnerved me. But I was enthusiastic and committed to helping these teenagers understand that to make a better world, we should learn to speak at least one other language. And I was here to teach them Spanish!

We did our repetition drills clearly and slowly. As they tried to parrot back credible accents and master sentence structures, I could see them droop with fatigue and frustration. They did not sense anything real about our practice. I asked myself what could I do to excite them. I could travel to Spanish-speaking countries and bring back authentic pictures and posters, audiotapes and records. But it was still just me importing something artificial into the classroom.

Then things began to change. As Spanish-speakers increased in numbers in the country, recognition of their culture grew. A teenage singing group, Menudo, reached the top of the charts. Spanish TV programs and stations began to appear, movie sound tracks were available in Spanish and there were audiotapes and CDs of salsa and *son*. Crossover stars Ricky Martin (Menudo now grown up) and Gloria Esteban were on MTV, as well as regular broadcast shows. Young people had easy access to Spanish-speaking media. Gradually, learning to speak Spanish was no longer an exotic goal; it was inviting, fun, and necessary for future communication.

Retirement came and I could rest. Future students would be more willing to pursue their studies of foreign language. Teachers would be well supplied with convincing and lively materials. I was free to turn my attention elsewhere and began to teach special lessons for the Opera and Symphony. Last week I returned to an elementary school just across the street from the high school in which I taught my first classes. The young teacher greeted me smiling and advised, "Speak clearly and slowly. Most of these youngsters speak only Spanish."

March 2001

Fireball

Swirling, boiling,
red, orange and yellow,
round, not like a mushroom
like an explosion.......
of anger, of hate

Expanding, breathing,
but not giving life
taking it.......
foreboding the death
of hope, of trust

Dropping, falling,
a gray dust of ashes,
of destruction,
acrid smoke and shreds......
of lives lost and dreams crushed

September 2001

This Year

It's different now. In conversations with my friends we allude to it, but, through tacit agreement, do not dwell on it. The newspapers and magazines chronicle the recent events over and over again. The editorial writers skillfully put my thoughts into their words, and I shake my head in agreement as I read their columns. Suddenly all of us are fearful of so many things: flying in airplanes that might fall out of the skies, spores on our letters that can infect us, attacks on buildings, even men who wear beards.

Thanksgiving Day came and was sunny and warm. My family ate turkey, gave thanks for the plentiful food in front of us, and toasted our friends and family as always. Not I, nor any of us, spoke about our inner thoughts on this joyful occasion. But at some odd moment, the shadow of the fears that we are trying to keep hidden, pushed close to the surface.

The building contractor, working on a house down the street, drives a truck with an American flag painted on the side and a handwritten tribute to his mother-in-law whose life was lost in the Pentagon; the young Air Force pilot who lives across the street is sent to Saudi Arabia to fly missions; the cable company representative on the phone whispers, in an aside, that her co-worker lost her mother that day; our daughter calls from New York City to describe the World Trade Center site, still smoldering, teddy bears, flowers, and mementos left, as if it were a war memorial. With each reminder I try to stop the horrific images from reappearing in my mind's eye. If I am successful and forget for a day or two, I feel guilty because I am letting the memory fade.

I want the Christmas season to start early this year. I look forward to the endless carols in the shopping malls, and I can't wait to join the crowds that I, as well as the serious economists, hope will come to shop mindlessly, from the Friday after Thanksgiving up until late evening on Christmas Eve. I will look for twinkling lights all over the houses in my neighborhood, the plastic snowmen, banners and flags with poinsettias, reindeer with red noses, candy canes, and as many garlands and holly, cut-out Santas and elves as the houses can bear.

I want to look in wonder, laugh at how theatrical and sensational the decorations are, drag out of our garage every accumulated decoration we have, and add green and red lights. I want to create a "winter wonderland" in our front yard, even if it doesn't snow on time. I will wait for the carolers who I hope will come, and play all the Christmas CDs I own over and over again. If I keep my mind busy creating a dream world, then I won't have time to dwell on the world in which we live.

Shortly after Christmas Day this incomprehensible year will be over. The sun will start its journey back, and as the days grow longer, I will resume the routine that was interrupted so traumatically four months ago. But there will not be the same carefree feeling. This year is different. And so will be the future.

December 2001

Summer 2002

A drive into downtown reveals that the grass along the parkway has gone dormant and is turning brown. The young saplings planted in great anticipation of the growth of their shady crowns get the wrong message and begin changing colors thinking that autumn has come. The river has receded from its banks, and the herons sit uncomfortably on the mud flats while the ducks waddle laboriously out towards the shallow water. A pair of mallards give up on the river and take up residence on our lawn when they discover they can get a shower from our sprinkler system.

We go to the pool seeking to rejuvenate with a quick dip. The poolside walk is so hot I have to run to the edge of the pool and jump in before my feet start to sizzle. And then I find my swim feels like a bath in tepid water. At break time, the ice cream man hands me a popsicle, all smoky and frozen hard, but it begins to melt immediately and starts to drip down my hand.

We retreat into our air-cooled houses and shut the door to the outside. The heavy air and listless feeling follow us inside. We perspire even while sitting quietly with a book on our lap. The dog senses that the temperature outside is not fit for beasts and will barely struggle up from his position under the ceiling fan to go outside to follow the call of nature.

"It must be global warming," we say, or "el Niño or la Niña." We don't recall any summer as hot as this one, though our weathermen tell us there have been. We muse about the English diplomats sent to our city who were given a hardship allowance before air conditioning was common.

A thunderbolt jumps out of the sky and explodes along the trunk of a tree in our yard. "Can a rain storm be brewing?" We press our faces against the window to look at the sky, scanning for flashes, listening for thunder. We can see the pulsations of heat lightning, but know the phenomenon will come to nothing. Some drops fall. They are too large and stop short of bringing any relief to our parched neighborhood.

Patiently, willing away our lethargy, we wait for the shorter daylight hours of autumn. We look forward to longer shadows and lower temperatures and a quenching rainfall...and to the welcome realization that this summer has come to an end.

August 2002

Washington Winter 2003

"We look forward to longer shadows, lower temperatures, a quenching rainfall.....and to the welcome realization that this summer has come to an end" (Essay "Summer 2002," written in August of 2002)

It was a long dry summer that exhausted us from our efforts to stay cool and be productive in our pursuits. Yet, looking backwards through the pages of the calendar, our worry about the weather seems inconsequential and even slightly whimsical. We fretted about our brown lawns, but serious anxiety about the consequences of a sustained draught never rose to any great proportions.

In the early autumn, our sensitivities were stirred by the one-year anniversary of the attack on the World Trade Towers. The media replays of that terrible day in September 2001 made us close our eyes and will our minds not to see the horror anew each night as we prepared for sleep. Intensive security preparations to protect us from any violent incidents that would mark the date were successful, and we did not suffer any new traumas.

Until October. Suddenly it seemed that gas stations, schoolyards, the very bushes across the street from our grocery stores, harbored potential danger, maybe even death. "Not a terrorist," they said, "just a sniper." "A sniper?" we mused. We had heard of snipers but they seemed to exist only in war novels and films. Our latent fears of terrorism were stirred as we avoided certain stores and locales, only to suspect that a new place, perhaps the one we were in, would be the next chosen location. Our relief was mixed with amazement when the young boy and his controlling partner were arrested while sleeping in a dirty blue car. Perhaps now we could relax. We were safe.

We celebrated Thanksgiving and Christmas, got on with our lives, though always alert to terrorist attacks across the world. We had some light snow that seemed to extend the Christmas feeling, and grumbled about delayed flights and planes that had to be de-iced. The snow kept coming. Global warming did not seem quite as frightening. Snow days off from school and late business openings made every week a holiday week. The snow did not stop, and almost as if to divert our attention from an advancing war effort, we found ourselves buried in a real blizzard. Folks from the north probably laughed at our bewilderment, but we rallied. We found our snow boots from the back of the closet, dusted off our snow shovels and sleds, and had a roaring good time acting as if we lived in the Yukon. And how we complained when the rain that followed turned our wonderland into a soggy mess! (How fickle we are about rain.)

The undercurrent of fear returned shortly when we were warned about religious celebrations that might trigger attacks on our homeland. We hurried about trying to make ourselves safe, while feeling foolish about our very preparations. Some of us took everything quite seriously but wonder if our piled-up supplies are really worth anything other than a nervous laugh.

So many days of this dark season have held a surprise. And now we are at war. Still the seasons have changed, unobtrusively, with a day and night of equal length. We see signs of renewal in the early purple crocuses, the tiny yellow snowdrops, and the chorus of birds who can find seeds easily now. Our attention will be captured by the soon to flourish cherry blossoms and flowering pear trees. We will look away from our TV screens and newspaper headlines to nature's beauty to find solace from the disturbing winter that has just past.

early March 2003

The Potomac River
Washington, D.C.

Rain

"Rain, rain, go away. Come again another day." It will soak through my thick wooly coat to the skin, the bushes will get my face all wet when I pass by, and the scents that I follow will be muted. But, a walk is a walk and, rain or not, I am glad that my companion is willing to strike out into the misty, cool morning.

She urges me to run into the raindrops and seems to like the spray in her face. She isn't watching me. She is looking at the wet, brown and leafless tree limbs that seem to form a pencil-sketch against the gray sky. She points to a formation of low-flying geese honking overhead and tells me that those lazy birds are heading for the local golf course and have told their leader to land quickly so they can eat. The crows are flying about too and, as usual, are quarreling noisily.

Her eyes can see the muted shades of green as we stroll past bamboo and mountain laurel that grow prolifically in our neighborhood. The crimson berries on the holly must be special for her because she often pauses to stare at the branches that hang low. Something has caught her eye. It's just a little bird. But she calls it a cardinal and is excited at its royal red coloring.

I see only shades of gray and black, but as wet as I know I will get, I think I'll push into the undergrowth to scratch my head and back on the branches. Maybe I will find a squirrel rummaging in the fallen leaves. Nothing. I think squirrels don't like rain very much either. I see a puddle at the curb and will have a drink. She likes to kick the water gently and listen to its soft sounds.

When we get home she will towel me dry and make herself a cup of coffee. The aroma makes the house feel warm and secure. We will sit together for a moment in front of the terrace door and look at the hazy panorama from our house on the hill. She says that the overcast sky means the rain will continue for a while. She has lots of things to do; she is such a busy friend. But, for this moment she is tranquil, content to linger and move in slow motion. This rain is not so bad after all, and I beg her with my eyes to stay next to me, silent and still, until it goes away.

February 2001

Small Pleasures

My calendar is filled with activities; my computer beckons me to sit down and write. I am endlessly busy and rarely pause to savor the day and enjoy the passage of time. "Slow down!" says my inner voice. I don't take advantage of that sensible advice very often, yet occasionally something catches my attention and my pace slows.

There are deer in the neighborhood who are elusive and seek cover under the brush easily found on streets other than ours. But I know their nocturnal secret. In the meadow behind our house they lie sleeping, silently and safely in the darkness. On early walks, I find the long meadow grass molded into a giant nesting place where, because of the warm bodies that have been resting there, there is no morning dew.

The river and local golf course provide a haven for the lazy Canada geese who just won't fly home. The large flocks of feeding geese are everywhere but my attention is caught by the several, self-appointed guardian geese. One or two heads are up, alert, ready to sound an alarm if danger is perceived. Their protective instinct is impressive, and I take a moment to contemplate the power of trust, even among animals. In a nearby marsh, standing motionless, is another friend. Looking like a shaggy dog sitting on a pole, a blue heron watches quietly, perched on one leg. I call him Mr. Blue, and greet him with a smile and wave.

When it rains the minutes seem to slow down, and as long as I can hear the sound of the drops falling, there is no haste in the passage of time. I can write, read and drowse. I can sit on the covered balcony with a cup of coffee with my woolly dog who also loves the cool, moist air. After the rain is the best moment when the air is freshly washed, the leaves are still dripping, and the sky is slowly clearing.

The busy year passes by quickly. Nevertheless, the Christmas season never comes too early for me. I take my favorite holiday CDs into the car on Thanksgiving day, and the lyrics that evoke thoughts of snow, mistletoe, and holly, delight me. The recordings of fine choral groups, the albums of the old-timers – Bing Crosby, Andy Williams, Perry Como – bring back memories of childhood excitement and anticipation. During this festive season, the small pleasures evoked by the music, the twinkling lights, the wintry scenes on greeting cards, and the anticipation of celebrating with friends and family multiply into a joyous array. Now my hectic pace seems to have a focus. I may never slow down enough, but each passing day is exhilarating and filled with the many delights of the season.

Christmas 2003

A blue heron on the Virginia shoreline
Potomac River

To Be Perfectly Honest

I want to say
that I am totally freaked out
when someone tells me
they are going to be perfectly honest.

It's like "Whoa!"
Can I believe what they told me
before declaring their honesty?

Whatever...
I guess when they are in
that particular mood,
they can also be totally frank.

Totally.

So I will be honest with you.
I feel like I need to say
that I hate clichés.....really,
and try not to use them myself.

I like to think out of the box
and well, duh.......be a creative person.
I hope that at the end of the day,
I will be able to express myself
using original phrases.

Stay tuned.

January 2003

"Pull Here"

Is it age or is it that things are just plain harder to open? A jar used to require a sharp tap on a hard surface to break the vacuum seal, a brisk twist... and it was open. Nowadays, there is some sort of shrink-wrapped seal over the edge that requires a sharp-tipped knife to cut through at the exact spot where the top meets the neck of the jar.

Pill bottles are yet another story. No matter how many times I request that the pharmacist give me a regular cap, I get the safety one. So I have mastered the skill of pressing and turning simultaneously... most of the time.

Wait! A new safety cap has appeared. This one requires pressing down tabs that are on both sides of the bottle, while turning the top with what? Your palm? It is a small bottle I might add, hardly worthy of my adult-sized hand. I call for help, and my husband arrives to show his true worth, he grabs the bottle, encircles it with massive palm power, and with a mighty grunt, gives a twist. The cap flies off. All that remains now between me and the pills is that aluminum seal (my sharp-tipped knife to the rescue) and the cotton that is firmly packed in the neck (thank goodness for my tweezers).

If a small bottle can defeat me that easily, those small plastic packages that read "Tear here" hold a special terror. You know what I mean. At every fast food place the cashier always points you to the bins that hold little packets of catsup, mustard, mayonnaise, and relish.

I like a little mustard on my hot dog, so I grasp the package, squint to find the tiny nick that shows where the weakest point is, and tear. Nothing happens. Okay, time for my teeth. No use. Now, my teeth and fingers. Maybe it opens with a squish and the ingredients run down my face. If I am still unlucky, I search for a sharp instrument among all the dull plastic utensils. Sometimes the serrated edge of a plastic knife will do it. If not, I search my purse for a nail file, or look so unhappy that someone finally offers to help me.

I also like cream, or half and half, in my coffee. Yes, you know that I am referring to those tiny cups with a tabbed seal on top. Well, how do you do it? I grab the tab and gently pull. If still nothing happens, I pull more firmly, but I have to grab the cup a little tighter. Now, without understanding much about physics, I do know that if I squeeze too tightly I will reduce the size of the container, and when the top seal is broken, the cream will just have to find a place to go. Whoops!

Time for breakfast and I want to try a new cereal. The "Open here" doesn't open here, but rather at some point that tears up the rest of the cover of the box. Now it is impossible to close the top in any way other than by shoving the whole top into the box. Next, how do you get into the bag that holds that wonderfully fresh, sealed-in flavored cereal? Out comes my favorite knife. This time I jam the tip down into the box as I grab the waxed bag so that I can pierce it. Okay, with a rush of fragrant cereal-perfumed air, it opens. Will it ever close again? Doubtful. Is there any way to save the freshness of this morning's cereal? I don't think so. I use more of my shoving technique and ignore the sound of the bag puffing open under the severely damaged top.

The challenge doesn't stop. What is the secret to get into the shrink-wrapped cover of a CD? The wrap sticks with a mighty static cling to all sides of the plastic case. The sharpest tip is needed. Sometimes I have to go to my desk to find my exacto knife. Even after that lethal pointed tip cuts a nice slice in the surface, the wrapper resists removal. The parts that do come off stick to my fingers and clothes and make completing the job a serious wrestle between me and the forces of static electricity.

Finally, the wrapper is off. What now? An adhesive seal with, you guessed it, a "Pull here" message. I pull. And the message, but not the seal, comes off in my hand. Not wanting to scratch the cover, first I try my fingernails and sheer persistence to pull the adhesive line off the side closure. I generally need the exacto knife again. I am finally ready to open the cover now. My perfected squeeze-and-pull movement must be properly executed. If just one tiny piece of the plastic wrapper or the adhesive seal still remains, I am left tugging and swearing at the ridiculous difficulty of getting into this CD.

Is it a conspiracy? Can we file a class-action suit charging mental anguish against... against whom? Or, shall I just sit back, sheath my knives, and enjoy the music from that CD. Maybe I'll have a cold drink to sooth my nerves now that I have gotten this off my chest. Let's see what's in the fridge. There is just the thing I want in a frosty pop-top can. Just grab the tab and pull here...

May 1995

Ballet Class

(then)

I can't wait until school is over, and finally I can race home, grab my dance bag, and run to the bus stop. It is time for ballet class.

I like going to school, especially during the times when we are allowed to read any book we choose. But I get so tired of sitting still. I wonder why we have to be still for so long? To me, the best time is when I can run to the school building, up all the steps, and slide into my desk just before the bell rings. And then I can walk home for lunch and repeat the run back to start the afternoon lessons.

The bus that will take me to the ballet school can't come quickly enough for me. When I get off, I race to the end of the next block, trying to run faster than the bus can move. My favorite driver laughs because he can't drive past the traffic lights and into traffic faster than I can run. I always win.

If I have enough breath, I continue running past the shops on the main street. Sometimes I slow down because I like to look into the windows. There is the barbershop where I get my hair cut, the Five and Dime store that sells all that junk, and the bakery where I can always see little cakes baked in animal shapes to celebrate the coming holiday.

I have to walk down a long alley to the back of the dance studio where the dressing room is. I dress as quickly as I can in the flowery dance outfit my mom made for me. One day I want to wear a black leotard like the professional dancers, but for now the flowers are okay. I am always early, so it is fun to watch the class before mine finish up. They are little kids, and they haven't learned how to look graceful just yet.

It's time for my class to begin. I am always the first at the barre, ready to go when our teacher starts the lesson. She looks old to me because her face and hands are wrinkled. Her hair stands out in a big pouf and is coppery red. She is forceful and seems a little crazy. She doesn't use the real ballet terms that are French, I think, but tells us to point our feet in fifth position and so on. Even so, she makes us believe that she knows everything there is to know about ballet.

It is a magical moment for me when we hear the first notes and start our exercises. The piano player is the sister of a friend of mine and it is a mystery to me how she can play music she has never seen before. The melodies of the ballet music and the rhythm of our barre routine make me feel as if I am in another world.

The best part of the class is after the barre when we do leaps and jumps. I feel as light as the wind, and I think I can almost fly! There is a photo of a dancer in the studio, and it seems as if she is flying through the air. I know just how she feels when she leaps like that. But I always have trouble doing the exact steps that we have to remember in a dance pattern. And it is so hard to stay on balance until the music ends. Will I ever learn the discipline that is so strict? I wonder if I can ever become a professional ballerina?

Ballet Class
(now)

I am buoyed by the thought of the coming evening when school is over and it is finally time for me to go to ballet class.

I like my job, especially when my students seem able, at least for a minute, to speak a little of the language I am trying to teach them. But it is a fatiguing job that keeps me on my feet all day. I am glad that I am not sedentary, but I would like to be able to sit and relax a little, especially as the years pass and I feel wearier at the end of the day.

I must be crazy! I am complaining about being weary but longing for the moment when I will push my poor muscles even further than I do during the daytime. Yes, I can't wait for the moment when I will be able to bend and stretch, point my toes, and move as the music commands.

I have always loved ballet class. I can still remember running to class as soon as school was over when I was very young. I stopped dancing briefly when it seemed unseemly for a suburban working mother to run off to ballet class. I resumed dancing after a brief fling with aerobics. Somehow the aerobic exercise class did not seem graceful enough. I hated the stomping and sweating.

I see the other women dressed in leotards and tights. No, we are not professionals, but the studio has a dance company and we all follow the tradition of the uniform. It makes us feel serious about our dancing even though most of us wear short skirts and a shirt to cover the slight bulges we are acquiring. I try to do some warm up exercises, but we are not so serious and mostly we talk.

I admire our teacher, an elderly man in very unfashionable clothes and shoes that look like they are made to wear for bowling. But I know that when he teaches, the memories and shadows of his professional past come back, and we see an athletic and graceful figure demonstrating for us.

We dance to recorded music that doesn't have the thrill of the piano that I remember. But rehearsal piano players are hard to find these days. Oh, it feels good to stretch at the barre. I can't kick as high as I used to, but I can still touch the floor with my gracefully extended fingertips. He uses French terms and I can figure them out because now I know French, and besides, my previous teacher taught me all the moves.

When we leave the barre for the center of the floor, before the leaps and turns, we are expected to perform some slow movements. Why can't I ever remember the pattern? I don't remember having this much trouble when I was young! Finally we are asked to do turns, pirouettes, across the floor and to add in some graceful leaps. I am not as light as I remember. And the others are complaining that they can't get the movements right. Our teacher makes gentle corrections and is as serious with us as if we are going to perform in front of an audience.

Yet we all know that we are here for a brief moment of pleasure. One or two of us, who have trained from childhood and retained the suppleness and skills necessary, might perform with the resident amateur company. But most of us come to dream and to remember the moments when, if only in our minds, we could fly and were real ballerinas training in our ballet class for our coming performance.

February 1997

"I Am A Musician"

It was mid-summer when I first heard the band. We were on our way to the neighborhood Fourth of July picnic, and hearing a familiar Sousa march, I began to walk a little faster, responding to the cadence. There was a time when I played clarinet in high school, and we played those same marches. Suddenly, happy memories of concerts and holiday parades came flooding back.

This July was different for me. I didn't have to think about returning to work in the fall because I had retired in June. I was content and anticipating a leisurely life style; yet, I was aware of a subtle fear that kept nudging me. For years, every day required my full attention and concentration. I was called upon to use my education, experience, and wits to manage a classroom and teach a foreign language. What would I do now with my time now that I did not have a daily commitment?

Excited by the music I wondered if I could still play the clarinet. It had been so many years since my high school days and then I had played with the marching band for only two years. The scholastic requirements of my college courses demanded all of my attention, and there was not enough time to fit in practices and performances with the university band. Now I wondered if I could ever be accomplished enough to play with a community concert band. I approached the director and he encouraged me, joking that "you just have to be able to carry your own instrument into rehearsals."

My own instrument. Did I have one? Perhaps my son had left his clarinet in a closet. I went home energized, and found it. It was not looking too bad for the years it had been resting, awaiting its next player. I assembled it, proud of myself for figuring out how all five parts fit together. I found the mouthpiece, a reed and the ligature with which to attach the reed. Could I play a note? My mouth had lost its firmness, and I seemed to be blowing hard enough to create a windstorm. But there it was, wavering, out of tune, but a real sound. My fingers were hesitant and the keys mysterious, but one by one I found other notes and a ragged scale emerged.

Lessons. I had to take lessons and that would mean finding a teacher and practicing everyday. I would be an adult learner, and my capacity to remember and progress would be slower than ever. How long would it take to become an acceptable clarinet player? How long to call myself a musician?

"Courage," I told myself and stumbled on with my newly discovered avocation. In the fall, I began to sit in on rehearsals and joined the community band that had first attracted me. I started using words like "gig" to describe performances, discussing the quality of reeds and their care, where to buy the best instruments and where to have them repaired. I consulted my fellow players about alternative fingering of notes, the best technique when reaching for the highest octave and how to tongue a staccato passage. We gossiped about the conductors in the area and about our acquaintances who play in various pit bands or swing ensembles.

Shortly, I could count numerous concerts in which I had played at retirement homes, picnics, Octoberfests, and in the town square. With these experiences added to my background, I bravely joined a larger concert band that is part of the local community college music program. Nowadays, I can proudly invite my friends and family to concerts performed on campus in a 1000-seat concert hall with impressive acoustics.

I have found other volunteer venues, a number of them related to my interest in music. Quite often I am asked to help assemble or tune an instrument. When I respond with a reasonable amount of expertise, my colleagues ask how I know how to do it. Usually I say, "Oh, I play the clarinet...I am an amateur." Lately, I just skip the details and tell them, "I am a musician."

February 2004

Senior Moments

"Stand up straight!"

Okay, okay, Mom! Will you stop it! I will stand up straight…for a while. But then, you and I know, the slump will appear again. And you will tell me that if I don't straighten up, I will never be able to.

I don't intend to walk as if I am afraid of my height. But, I am. I am taller than all of my friends. What really makes me scared inside and want to shrink is that I am taller than most of the boys I know. It's not that I want to date them, but I am awkward enough when I talk to them. Towering over them is impossible.

Mom, you married a tall guy, my father, and when I look at him, I am proud of his dignified bearing. His family is tall and slender, as am I and my brother, and I know that one day I will be proud to carry myself upright, in a full stance. It's just that, right now, I can't.

Okay, okay, Doctor! I will make a resolution to stand up straight and tall and will try to walk that way for an hour, for a whole day...for the rest of my life. I will do the exercises you gave me, hold my head upright, and watch myself in the mirror until I have got it just right.

I married a man who is my same height. These days, I can even talk comfortably to my colleagues who are shorter than I. I believe the reports say that many of the most successful people are tall. I am ready to draw myself up to my full height and flaunt it.

How tall am I? Let me measure myself. No, don't say that...that we shrink as we grow older. Does that mean that, finally, now that I am proud of my stature and determined to follow the instructions I have heard all of my life to "stand up straight," I can't attain my full height?

Mom, were you right?

August 2000

"This Wheelchair Feels Good"

Finally we are here. It took two flights totaling 15 hours of flying time to get us to this ancient city, Beijing. We are still suffering from jetlag but the excitement of visiting the Forbidden City has sent enough adrenaline through our veins to make us raring to go. I am, that is. My partner doesn't look as peppy as he usually does. Well, the photographic opportunities will revive him shortly.

Tiananmen Square does not disappoint us. We pass through the gates of the City gaping at the mural of the Chinese ruler and begin our trek through the endless courtyards. It is not a hard walk, but something is happening to my mate. Instead of perking up, he seems to be walking with a list. I'll take his heavy camera bag. That might help.

Our tour guide is watching him and me. Should I say something to her? First, we must have our picture taken to preserve our special moment here at this historic site. He is standing up straight for the occasion; maybe everything is okay. Before I can approach her, our guide comes over and inquires about his vision and tries to determine if he is lucid. Though she does not use the words that suggest a catastrophic health event, she suggests that we borrow a wheelchair for him. He agrees, and as he lowers himself into the chair, sighs, "This wheelchair feels good."

A wheelchair? In my mind, wheelchairs are for people who are old and infirm. I am terrified of what is happening at the moment and of the future that threatens to confine us to moving about encumbered by one. Is this just a brief moment that with good doctoring will pass? Or is this a view of our life to come?

We drive through the city while I pray that he stays conscious and coherent. The hotel staff is helpful, and we are taken to a health clinic where the doctor can monitor his heart rhythm and blood pressure. He is stable though his malady is of an unknown cause. We are advised to return home and given information on obtaining wheelchairs at each stopover.

Once home, we are relieved to be told that the episode was caused by malaria contracted many months before and left undiagnosed. He has recovered...but have I? The dismay of hearing a loved one admit that he needs to use a wheelchair still haunts me.

August 2000

"You Look So Young!"

It must be my hair that elicits the comment. I have been favored by nature, and it still looks black with just a small hint of gray. It is the one part of my body about which I have not complained at any time. And it seems to be favoring me now.

But, what about those other body parts that work less smoothly as each day passes? When I study the movements of young people, I see that they move fluidly and effortlessly while bending and stooping, sprinting, and running. They don't follow the rules of bending their knees when lifting nor of swinging their legs out of the car before standing. They just stoop down and bounce up again, extend one foot out of the car and jump out onto it, and most amazing of all, they can spring upright out of a soft chair with no support from their arms and hands.

When did I stop moving that way? I can remember favoring my knee for a short time, but I am certain that I resumed my former flexible movements after the injury healed. I have always been able to arch and rotate my back with ease but it does ache sometimes, and maybe I avoid some twists and turns. I don't always sit up straight until the rearview mirror in my car reminds me that if I don't assume the proper posture, I will have to adjust it if I want to see the traffic behind me. If I sit down on the floor, getting up is a study in rolling onto my knees and hands and then pushing up in as dignified a way as my awkward position will allow.

I wonder how much longer I can fool the world into thinking I am younger than my years. I am searching out exercises to stretch out my back, to strengthen my upper body, and to maintain my flexibility. Suppressing the urge to groan, I will practice those maneuvers that seem so effortless for the young.

I know all of these tactics will be good for my health, but it is vanity that drives me. One day my hair will turn gray. Will I be able to distract attention away from my appearance and direct it towards my athletic and flexible moves? And, will I continue to hear that happy and lyrical phrase, “You look so young!”

August 2000

Age Spots

I thought they would show up on my hands first. That's where I have always seen them on older folks. That would be okay, at least until I could get used to the idea. They could be mistaken for freckles or moles there from birth, and if any caused the doctor to be suspicious, they could be removed without anybody noticing. But I have no reason to worry because I am not "old."

What, then, is that spot on my face? I've seen some tiny dots there for awhile and asked the doctor to check my face last month. This morning, that dot has become a spot, right in the center of my cheek. No, wait. It is two dots that have come together and formed one large... can it be?... age spot.

I should try to conceal this imperfection on my face. What shall I do? Cover it with heavy makeup? No, makeup might wear off later in the day. Maybe I should make it more prominent with a mascara pen. Then people will think I have intentionally put the spot there and it is a fashion statement.

They will be wrong! I don't like having everybody who looks at my face know that in spite of my protestations, I am aging and I don't relish the realization that I will have to follow seriously this spot's progress. What a great scenario. If I have it removed, I will have a small scar on my face. If it is of no concern to the doctor and is left there, it will probably enlarge.

Can I bargain for some spots on my hands, or even arms and legs, in exchange for adjusting my attitude towards the aging process? I promise to be more respectful and declare them to be not age spots but a sign of character and individuality. That sounds good...but I think I'll check my face one more time to see if maybe today, by some miracle, the spots have shrunk just a little bit.

August 2000

Faces

Most mornings it is the same, unchanging face that stares at me from my mirror. Busy with my morning routine, I am soothed by the familiarity of the face and the eyes that gaze back at me. Not too lively at this hour in the morning, still they are focused and clear. Luckily, being female, I can put a little concealer under each eye to cover some slight shadows, plus some rosy blush on my lips so I will have a healthy glow. I'm ready to go and feelin' good!

Occasionally I catch a glance of that same face in another mirror, maybe in a restaurant bathroom or in a clothing store, where the lighting is not flattering. And then I see another person. This one is an older person who has worry lines in the center of her forehead. Her chin is not so firm, and in spite of a very slender facial profile, there is the faint but definite beginning of jowls underneath the jawbone. The full head of hair, that seemed as if it would stay forever dark, has a slight graying cast to it.

Apprehensive as I am in these revealing moments, I recognize that I am not alone. I have heard the doleful complaint of friends who catch sight of themselves in a store window and are startled because they think they are seeing their own mother or father. A good friend who was so happy to have lost a few pounds from her frame, nevertheless complains, "To my eye, my face really looks older. All the droops are droopier, and I see the beginning of not just lines but wrinkles afflicting the whole of the left side."

In a pensive moment, I dwell on photographs of my friends and family taken over the years. How did those faces change ever so slowly from the photo that appears in a high school annual or in wedding day photos to today's rendition of those familiar faces? And how did my face become today's version? No matter how often I check my face in my familiar bathroom mirror, I can never see the changes take place.

And yet it is inevitable that my features will change. I like the phrase "older but wiser" and scan my face in those unexpected revealing moments to see if the years of experience, of skills mastered, and of history endured can be read in my face or in my eyes. I am content if my good health and happy spirits dominate my features though I recognize that those occasional moments of frustration, worry or sad thoughts are part of the range of a full life. Perhaps I will never able to detect the slow changes that occur in the face that greets me each morning. Nonetheless, when they do appear...may I always greet them with grace.

January 2003

Blue

"Why don't you pamper yourself and go to a salon for a haircut?" I asked my mom one day when she came to visit the grand kids. "You have lovely thick and wavy hair. I know my hair stylist would love to cut and shape your hair because it is so luxurious. She could make it easy to manage and cut it in a way that would make it fall attractively around your face, and we could ask what she would advise about using a rinse that will make any incoming gray hair sparkle and shine."

Mom froze. "What did you say? Cut and color my hair? Use a rinse? Don't you know that it will look like a blue helmet? I don't want to look like those ladies who play cards in the retirement village!"

"No, Mom," I protested. "It won't look stiff nor blue. It will look styled and fashionable. And the silvery tones will enhance how pretty and full your hair is."

As daughters do, I reminded my mom of my suggestion periodically. It became one of those mother-daughter dialogues that go on endlessly with neither listening to the other. My dad often joined the discussion, really an argument, supporting my mom. Neither she nor he would bend to the fashion world, feeling that fancy styling is frivolous and that using rinses is artificial. In fact, they implied that it is downright silly to try to improve on nature.

Now I am about the age that my mom was at the time of our discussions. I still go to the same hair stylist, and she cuts and shapes my hair. She colored my hair for a few years at my request because I told her that I did not want to appear "old."

I reconsidered when I retired and stopped the tinting entirely. It did seem...well, not so silly but definitely artificial. So she suggested a natural shampoo that would highlight my increasingly graying hair. It had a lovely fragrance, and I purchased a small bottle. The next day, I opened the bottle in the shower and poured a tiny bit of it into my hand. It was blue.

December 2001

“How Are You?”

There was a time when that simple question was easily asked, and the equally easy answer was: “I’m fine, thank you. And you?” Conversation could then begin and friends could explore personal questions slowly and gently as the telephone call or dinner date progressed.

But somehow, nowadays, after a brief “hi” or “hello,” conversational partners seem eager to inform you that their colon has been thoroughly examined, or maybe it is that they have to take preventative medication when they won’t be near a bathroom. Male friends are happy to report that their prostate has been prodded and my female friends willingly share tales of their mammogram. Other times I am addressed, in a whisper, about a convenient product that allows one to maintain one’s poise and confidence while away from facilities for extended time periods.

Yes, my companions are aging as am I along with them, and discussions about our health do take up more and more time in our conversations. And I suppose it is good to discuss common problems. My closest friend and I have shared our thoughts in what we call our “ten year discussion of hormone replacement.” We gave each other a collegial pat on the back when recent information confirmed our suspicions about the horrors of long-term usage. And we always compare our weight and cholesterol figures and cheer companionably when either drops.

But I ask, do I really need to know how lumpy the breasts are of an acquaintance at the pool or exactly which vertebrae aches in her battle of advancing osteoporosis? I am always happy when a lingering health problem is solved, but I would rather skip the discussion of toenails that are no longer purple thanks to a miracle fungal medicine.

Why does the simple "How are you?" elicit a stream of personal health information these days? Is it because our exchanges are more and more hurried, and in these advancing years, our physical problems more numerous? Do we feel that we must rush to get in all of the details before the brief conversation is over? Or perhaps the well-rehearsed greeting no longer conveys a feeling of sincerity. I do like the query and hope my friends will continue to inquire as to how I am. However I promise not to mention my aching back, my bowel, bladder, breasts or colon...at least until we have shared some convivial moments together.

August 2002

Now, Where Did I Put My Keys...?

Usually they are in my coat pocket where I put them when I come home, and they are easy to find, but sometimes they just seem to have a mind of their own and "hide" in unlikely places. I find them under folded clothes that I have taken off before going to sleep, inside one of my shoes, under my bed, or sometimes in a drawer. I certainly didn't put them in any of those places.

Our wireless telephones seem to share a similar mindset. They must know that they will disappear periodically because they have a paging system and signal where they are if I press the button on the base. My cell phone is even more ornery because it is small and can hide in the tiniest spaces under the car seat or between cushions.

So why am I looked at curiously when I conduct my search and rescue missions? It doesn't matter to me that the keys were in the wastebasket or the refrigerator. Eureka! I am just happy to find them. It is not only because of my misplaced articles that I receive looks of pity. If I take a wrong turn on the way to a friend's house, forget the map, the address, or phone number, my soundness of mind is questioned.

Young people can get away with lost articles and other woes, and they are excused for being distracted or having more important things on their mind. I have young friends who have left keys in locked cars with the motor running, forgotten combinations to locks, lost the locks themselves, and packed passports into suitcases that are unreachable because they have been checked-in. In one extraordinary case, a young acquaintance pressed the gas pedal instead of the brake and saw first-hand how an air bag can protect the head from hitting the dashboard.

Why are we aging folks held under such strict scrutiny? For any of the above slips, my friends would counsel me to look into retirement homes where the management rescues its elderly residents from mishaps. And, they would certainly suggest that I take the "55 and Alive!" driving course.

Oh well, I know I can stay ahead of that aging curve. My years of experience have provided me with wisdom, and I know how to troubleshoot! I will look first in my shoes for my keys, I will call my cell phone with the wireless phone, and I will put my lists and maps right under my purse. Okay, I am done whining for the moment and am leaving to go to the grocery store.

Now, where is my purse?

December 2001

Strolling

While strolling leisurely, each morning
with my giant companion, Bear,
we push farther away, with each step,
our common condition.....
senior citizenship.

From his first days with us,
large breed that he is,
we knew his life span would be short;
he would quickly catch up with me,
and we would become "seniors" together.

We started walking in the early morning,
loping along, making an aerobic activity
out of our morning mile.
But his style convinced me that stopping
and taking time to breathe deeply,
to observe, to ponder a little,
was more satisfying.

Now, as we both age,
he, a little faster than I,
we stop and start, and arrive home
a bit weary but ready for our day to come,
he, doing what dogs do..... sleep,
and I, what retired folks do..... volunteer.

We are feeling quite well for our ages and
look forward to our morning stroll together.
Except for an occasional groan from him
when he sits down on the floor
or an audible sigh from me when I kneel to garden,
we greet our day with enthusiasm.

August 2003

"Bear"
A Newfy mix, age 10

Across the Footlights

I've finished putting together my clarinet; my stand is in place and the music is in order. My reed is moistened, and I am ready for the downbeat. Pleased at this new venture, I feel energized by the occasion. Having renewed a skill that dates back to my high school days, from the very first performance in which I played, I have felt a sense of surprise and delight to find myself onstage, facing an audience, as a member of a concert band.

When I retired from teaching seven years ago, I had no plans for the future. Leisure time, no deadlines, sleeping a little later in the morning and waking unhurriedly, would mark the rhythm of my life. But perhaps, I reasoned, I should find some challenging activity to keep my mind active. Maybe music. In the closet there was a clarinet abandoned by my son. Could I once again play it?

I have a moment to glance across the room at the gathering audience. They move slowly, with the halting grace of aging bodies. Some walk companionably close to one another as if for support. Others lean on canes or walkers. There are a few wheelchairs. It will be a pleasurable evening for them as they listen to some light classics, a few bright marches, and a short overture. Some will sway to the rhythm or mark the beat with their hands. Others, after sitting quietly for a few minutes, will drift off to sleep.

They are an affluent crowd who live in this retirement community. Many were professionals in their working years and led productive lives, some of them living in other countries. They have listened to the world's best orchestras performing in the grand music halls of the world, active and able for many long years. Slowly, as their strength waned, they have retreated to this safe haven. Now they sit contentedly, waiting for us to begin. When they hear the sounds of the music we play, what sweet memories will float through their minds?

Our director approaches the podium; we come to order and raise our instruments, ready to perform. The audience quiets in anticipation. In the brief moment before we begin, I study the faces I can see beyond the lights. Some await with smiles of pleasant expectation, others are intent upon hearing the first notes. Perhaps one or two of them were musicians and know the tension and thrill of this moment. I flex my fingers, breathe deeply, and reflect for a brief moment on the thought that one day, perhaps, I will sit where they are, across the footlights.

June 2003

Misty

The concert hall is dimly lit. The wooden panels that frame the back wall of the stage glow softly under the few lights left on by the cleaning crew. The concert band members have not yet arrived to prepare for the evening concert. The stage is empty except for a solitary figure, barely visible, sitting in his assigned chair. He is an older man, formally dressed in concert attire. The saxophone held in his hands picks up a beam of reflected light. He plays, oblivious to his surroundings.

An instrumentalist enters from the back and stops still to listen to the single, melodious line of reedy notes. It is a mellow tune, written for a female voice but carried aloft this time by the golden resonance of the lovingly played saxophone. "*Look at me. I'm as helpless as a kitten up a tree...*"

The fluid notes float through the air. His rendition is sure as he cradles the instrument in his arms. Modulating his breathing, he coaches the vibrating reed into releasing clear, luminous tones into the air. "*And I feel like I'm clinging to a cloud I can't understand. I get misty just holding your hand...*"

It is a moment of reflection, of memories of past relationships. The sole listener recalls an earlier era when music and the pace of life were unhurried, and thoughtful pauses were more common. Just for a moment, time has stopped and the music calls up private recollections. "*Never knowing my right foot from my left... I'm too misty and too much in love...*"

The song ends. The listener, wishing to show appreciation for the special moment created by the musician, claps lightly. The spell is broken. The man stands, bowed as if accepting the applause, his posture clearly reflecting his advanced age. He explains, “I like to warm up with something other than scales.”

October 2002

White Head

"Beep, beep!" He looked in his rear view mirror and saw the young woman tapping insistently on her horn and gesturing for him to move on. They always did that. No matter how fast he moved after the light turned green, the person in the car behind always motioned or mouthed words in his direction, rudely urging him to move faster. Sometimes the gesture was just impatient, sometimes it was crude, and he guessed that it was the same for the words.

It wasn't that he didn't pay attention to the signals. He prided himself on staying alert, especially in traffic. It just seemed that there was no hurry to move. He knew that cross-traffic frequently raced through a red light, and it seemed safer to wait and move ahead with deliberation. Besides, it was easier to read the street names that otherwise tended to confuse him at higher rates of speed.

He noticed lately that it wasn't just in traffic that he seemed to move slower. From his first moments in the morning when he sat up in his bed, he needed more time. Early in his retirement he relished the extra moments in the morning. He liked not having to eat and dress in a rush and being able to read the paper carefully and completely. But lately the entire morning slipped away before he finished up and was ready to meet the day.

"Good," he reasoned. "I don't miss my work, especially the frantic schedule. And now I have time to do the things I enjoy leisurely." For a while he did that, indulging himself in phone conversations, reading, and conversations with people at the market and post office. And he stayed busy with occasional courses at the museum, helping out at the library, and filling in at local stores when the other employees were sick or on vacation.

His old colleagues called on him for advice and he liked sharing his knowledge and experience so much that they gave him the title of consultant. He was pleased because it reminded him of his importance to the company and of the prestigious position he once had as branch manager. He knew that the younger employees looked at him slightly humorously because he used terms that seemed old-fashioned to them. But he was confident that his information was worthy and time-tested, so he didn't pick up the new jargon just to impress them. He smiled silently to himself when these youthful faces complained about how much time they had spent mastering a work skill. He politely assured them, "Yes, you are certainly to be commended on your hard-earned expertise."

But slowly, as he became detached from current happenings in his field, his colleagues called on him less. He still went to the Christmas party but felt that the exclamations of "You look so good!" or "Retirement must certainly agree with you!" had replaced any meaningful conversation.

He still did look good, young for his age you might say. But he had stopped coloring his hair with that clever product on the market that gradually darkens hair and wears off slowly. He was pleasantly surprised to find that his white hairs sparkled under certain lights. He still had his closet full of clothes for professional occasions, but no occasion, except a dinner party or two, seemed worth dressing up for. He really liked his soft and worn sports outfits. Shopping never had been much fun for him, and with his small pension paycheck, he was secretly glad that he didn't have to spend much time looking for new clothes.

He did his regular exercises but preferred more and more the slow walks with his dog and a little bit of gardening around his house. His body was strong and surprisingly flexible. He was a little concerned that he could not spring out of chairs or the car as he once had. He understood that age does bring changes to the body and he tolerated the small aches and pains that came when he overdid some activity. He took painkillers, and as he had always done, tried not to give in to the annoying aches. He sometimes increased his vitamins but forgot them when he felt better.

He wondered how he would know the moment when, in spite of his vigor and mental acuity, he would be just an old man with white hair to those around him. Each day it seemed that the world was growing younger, and he felt diminished in that world. He didn't want to argue with those who beeped at him in traffic or tried to impress him with their knowledge. Neither did he want to become the "handsome oldster" that people chuckled at and he felt were demeaned by the well-meaning anchor on the morning TV show.

At the next light, he noticed that the young woman in the car behind was exceptionally pretty. He stepped on the gas just as the light turned green. Something stirred in him, and as he shifted down to hear the powerful grind of the motor, he thought about maybe coloring his hair just one more time.

November 1996

Old Men

Who are these old men
who live in our house,
who share our bed, and
who sit on our couch?

They squabble and quarrel,
they whine and complain,
they walk with a limp
they speak with disdain.

Their faces seem familiar,
maybe a bit old,
their hair has turned gray
their features less bold.

I think of the past
and it makes me sad,
because I think I recognize
these young lads...

Could they be the men
we dated and married,
who cause us to be
so weary and harried?

We are still young!
It isn't fair!
Why we wouldn't dare
squabble, quarrel,
whine and complain...

about these old men!

December 2000

Travel

Small Town – Home Town

The nearest airport is an hour away from their home, so just after landing, we are met by our son-in-law's parents who will drive us to their house. Graciously, with a European politeness, we are made to feel welcomed. As we drive along we notice that the towns seem to get increasingly smaller. And when we cross the line that marks the limits of Saint Agatha we begin to comprehend that we are in a town so small, population 900, it could be called a village. Though the access road bears a route number, it narrows down to two lanes, and we realize that village life hugs this artery. The traffic is mostly local and dominated by farm machinery and trucks. Passing a number of houses, we learn that our hosts' family and friends live in many of them. The car slows, turns right into a driveway, and we are "home."

Just behind the house is the lake that bears a name to match its size and shape – Long Lake. This summer day, it appears cool and calm; later in the day it will take on a rosy cast from the setting sun. There are loons, they say, but mostly it is the ducks and crows who create the noisy recital visitors hear during the day. Later in our visit we are shown ice huts tucked away under leafy trees for now but, in the winter, to be put on sleds and towed out to the center of the lake when it is frozen so friends and families can huddle together out of the wind and angle for fish through the ice.

In the morning, neighbors, who are also relatives, arrive by motorboat at the small wooden pier behind the house and offer to give us a tour of the lake. The day is warm but the wind generated by the speeding boat is cool and exhilarating. We cruise past a small island and can see summer homes that look luxurious but are too fragile to live in during the long, snowy winter. Gazing across the lake we see a broad panorama of pine forests, flowering fields in the distance, and a sky filled with graceful clouds. "Over there!" our hosts point at the village, nestled in a small cove carved out of the St. John Valley, marked by the school and several church spires. Now, as they chatter in their preferred language, French, they call their small town Sainte Agathe.

We are close to the Canadian border, in a region called Madawaska, the most northeasterly part of the state of Maine. It becomes clear to us why the tiny airport in Presque Isle is an international airport, as it lies just across the border from Edmundston in New Brunswick, Canada. Sainte Agathe, originally a Catholic parish settled by a group of French nuns known as the Daughters of Wisdom, was incorporated at the turn of the century. Madawaska takes its name from the local Iroquois Indian tribe, and we visitors to the area are reminded of the French and Indian struggles early in the 1700's.

Our new relatives take us to the house in which they raised their two children, the site of a still-operating grocery store. "I lived next to the lake all of my life, but I was always in the front of the store. Only now do I have a view of it from every room," says our son-in-law's mom, praising her new house located four miles down the road.

Hard working shopkeepers until just a few years ago, she and her husband still actively farm and cultivate potatoes (for which the area is famous) and other staples to stock their refrigerator. An agricultural community, school children are excused for two weeks in the fall so they can help with the potato harvest.

An evening barbecue is organized to celebrate the common birthdays of our daughter and son-in-law and is attended by all of the family members who live in town and some who have returned just for this occasion. Each brings a contribution to the meal, including homemade wine, and we are introduced to the sisters and brothers, aunts and uncles, cousins, and friends of this large, affable family who welcomes us as one of them. We meet the aunt who was at one time a Daughter of Wisdom, the young cousin who attends the local school, the uncle who lives in their grandmother's house, and the aunt who is the town's postmaster.

We easily adjust to our new, congenial environment, but shortly our visit is over. On our drive back to the airport we feel we have a new family now, whose members live in the tiny town to which they introduced us. We prepare to board the plane that will take us back to where we live, and as we hug them and bid them good-bye, we promise to return to what is now a town in which we feel at home.

August 2003

Long Lake
Sainte Agathe, Maine

An Aussie

He is a big man who wears levis, leather boots, and a bush ranger's hat, just as expected. His greeting is "G'day mates," and the day begins to resemble a scene from a "Crocodile Dundee" movie. But, however full of good humor and ready to relate anecdotal tales of his country, our Aussie guide wants to convey the true magnificence and reality of the island continent that is his home.

He loves what he calls "Australiana" and collects mementos from the past: books published years ago that record the history of his "*terra australis,*" medals that mark the building of the Sydney Harbour Bridge, and stories of the survivors of the awesome task of linking the two sides of the harbor. Daily, he takes visitors on ghost tours of the old city and plots how to ensnare them in his scary tales of the early history of his country.

Journeying to a cliff overlooking the bay, our guide spots the original entry channel that led the early sailors to the secure cove that became the Sydney harbor. From a harbor boat, he points out the landmark opera house, the bridge, and Circular Quay that marks that first cove. Walking through the botanical gardens, he laughs at the squealing fruit bats hanging upside down in a cluster of trees. At dinnertime we eat local "tucker' with him in waterfront restaurants. We hear about the convicts that came to Australia to make their new life there and who died and are buried throughout the city.

Our guide is more of a historian than the bushranger he appears to be. If he were one of that hearty breed of men, he would belong to the group who came to the island as free men. He honors their resistance to authority, hard-work ethic, and their bravado. One night, while traveling through the Outback on an overnight train, he sings lustily "Wild Colonial Boy," and "Waltzing Matilda."

He glories in the natural beauty of his country, and after flying north to Cairns, he gently encourages those who are swimmers to follow him into the waters over the Great Coral Reef to watch the multi-colored fish swimming among the pulsating fronds of living sea life.

Rising out of the central desert is the awesome monolith called Ayers Rock. Our guide introduces the local ranger who is accompanied by a native person. They explain, first in her language and then in English translation, aboriginal legends and how verbal history and laws are passed on to future generations. Later will come the information on how the native people of the continent, the aborigines, are asking for "reconciliation" with the white population.

One night our guide, now a gregarious friend, points to the Southern Cross overhead and teaches a foolproof way to find it. Another day he finds kangaroo babies that he calls a "joey" and encourages petting them gently and shaking their hand; he waits patiently giving time for endless photos of cuddly koalas. The trip draws to an end, and at a farewell meal, bottles of delicate local wine from the vineyards of his native land are shared. The plane leaves at dawn and with one last embrace, the invitation issued to him to visit our home in the U.S. is confirmed and our new Australian friend bids us, "Ooroo, see ya'."

Brian McDonald is a guide for
Australian History Promotions
Sydney, Australia

April 2000

And A Kiwi

Weary of travel and having gotten up before dawn, our Kiwi guide is solicitous and attentive as he tells his plans for the projected visit to his tiny nation. What sites and views await that have not already been seen in this portion of the South Pacific? Our guide is a slender man with a white, clipped beard. He wears a vest of fine Merino wool, sports an open collar, and looks like a college professor. Having seen so many exotic natural wonders already, the first questions are hard ones that challenge his sociologic and anthropologic knowledge.

He reveals that he is most interested in explaining how his country handles racial questions and is proud to relate that Maoris are part of every phase of his nation's contemporary life, including the government. He personally has been adopted into a Maori tribe, is proud of his dual heritage, and speaks one of his country's native languages. First on his list is a Maori welcoming ceremony. He coaches his visitors in the appropriate courtesies to be used during the program.

His country is tiny but there are many places to visit. From the international base for Antarctic Exploration at the airport to his charming hometown of Christchurch, our guide sets a rapid pace. His town is small, placid, and very English in nature. He loves its beauty and applauds the recent efforts to bring back native flora and fauna that were destroyed by the English settlers in the early years.

There are some things that can never be changed by man. Our guide arranges for train rides into gorges, a lake cruise to view the glacial lakes and fjords, and a helicopter ride to see snowcapped mountains and acres of wilderness. One night, there is a dinner party at the house of our guide's friends and away from the city lights, in the crisp fall evening of March, once again the southern cross is visible. He is elated that tonight the sky is so clear that the thick Milky Way is visible as a backdrop.

Sixteen time zones ahead of the U.S., he relates how the volcanic North and South islands have been buffeted by geological shifts and sit on the same "ring of fire" as Tokyo and the San Andreas fault. From a hilltop outside of Auckland, he points out the more than 50 volcanic cones on which the city sits and how the city straddles an isthmus and has harbors on both the Tasman Sea and Pacific Ocean. When he speaks of the America's Cup won this year in that very harbor by his countrymen, his eyes sparkle with glee.

Outside of the big city, he plans a route to display the rolling countryside, quiet, traffic-free small towns, and tranquil sheep and deer grazing. A boat ride on the open ocean is a search for a view of the royal albatross. Happy to find chicks in their nests, neither he nor the ship's captain can locate an adult, but he is pleased to discover families of seals lounging in the sun. A gourmand, he loses all sense of discipline when he can indulge himself in the local fish and oysters that are farmed in the lakes and bluffs. He is a wine connoisseur, and at the winery he selects the finest "Pinot Gris" that his country has to offer.

There is more that our guide wants to show us. However, our time to visit is over. He makes us promise to return, and we invite him to our homes. We hug our new friend and say, in the Maori words he taught us, "Kia ora," to wish him "Good health."

Malcolm Campbell is a guide for
Eco Tour and Guiding Services,
Auckland, New Zealand

April 2000

Sun and Ice

It is after midnight and I am restless. The drapes don't block out enough light, and my body clock thinks it is still afternoon. Quietly I walk to the window and try to catch a view of Mount McKinley. The peak is shrouded in clouds, but I can see the wide, snow covered base on the horizon. There is so much light on this longest day I consider taking a chair outside to read my book while my mate sleeps. Better not. In a few hours, when the clock tells us it is morning, we are to meet our group and fly over the glaciers that cascade down the mountainsides.

We are captivated by the landscape of Alaska. We have passed through moss and lichen covered tundra and taiga forests of sticklike pine trees called "sitka" by the early Russian traders. We have seen snowy mountains separated by fjords formed by the glaciers that have passed through and since melted. We have heard the sound of giant pieces of glacial ice moving and breaking off to fall into ocean. And we can see the remaining massive glaciers in the folds of the mountain ranges in this subarctic region.

We fly over McKinley's glaciers and try to comprehend their size, their age, and their perpetual presence. The crevices are blue, a phenomenon of the play of light waves explained to us by our pilot. Our attention is not on the scientific moment but rather on the impressive display of nature: snow and ice that never melt, storms that defy the climbers who try to reach the summit, and life that exists in the form of tiny ice worms, rain and fog that swirl around our helicopter.

On previous days we have searched for wild animals, but they hide during the warm days and defeat our efforts. The bears are waiting for the salmon to begin their upstream swim and the moose, shy and solitary, avoid our human presence and hide in the shady brush. We are glad the local population protects the wildlife in this area called Denali by the Native Americans. They will take the curious only in buses and boats in cautious, noninvasive, sightseeing trips. One rainy day we see baldheaded eagles and their giant nests. And, we watch humpback whales blow, breach, and dive while feeding, giving us a view of their giant tails, called flukes, just before disappearing below the surface.

The sled dogs pant even though their demonstration races are short. They await cooler weather to start their training for the 1100-mile Iditarod race from Anchorage to Nome. Gnawing on moose bones, they are happy while their trainer tells us about the snowy race. A small, almost delicate breed, their coat feels like tough bristles on our fingers. Their bright eyes tell us that they are happy to see us but would rather be working at their job of training to pull the sleds and gear through the ice fields.

We have passed through the tiny towns of the inner passage of fjords and rivers. These former gold rush towns can be accessed only by boat or plane and their populations are tripled when a cruise ship is in town. High school and college students, young members of their Native American clan, teach us about their families and how their ancestral communities have survived in this cold territory over the centuries.

The earth flourishes in mid-June, and we have to use our imagination to think of the darkness that comes in December. We squint against the glare of the sun that shines directly into our eyes during the endless afternoons and adjust our cameras knowing that the shadows are long and the brightness is deceptive. Today the sun gives us hours of light; tomorrow the day will be several minutes shorter. Soon we will leave this land of sun and ice for our own temperate climate to contemplate how life will change here during the long, snowy, icy nights to come.

June 2001

La Serenissima

A plane, a bus, a vaporetto* to take us to our stop on the Grand Canal, a phone call in Italian for street directions, and a trek along narrow streets dragging suitcases behind us does not seem like a very serene foreshadowing of our visit to Venice. Finally we are rescued by a helpful American who sensing our bewilderment, offers to guide us to the very doorstep of our hotel.

Even in our weary state we are aware of the picturesque gondolas gliding along in front of the waterside cafes and hotels. Our short walk introduces us to the tiny bridges that cross the numerous canals and the shops full of jewelry crafted from sparkling Murano glass, Carnival masks, candies and pastries, and pasta in shapes and colors we have never seen before. We know we are in a city that is more than twelve centuries old and built on islands connected by canals and bridges. There are no cars or bikes for us to dodge. What eludes us in these early moments of our visit is the tranquil and noble qualities promised by her reputation.

The next morning, after coffee and sweet rolls, we step out on the balcony overlooking the Grand Canal. The vaporetti that pass by, one right after another, are crowded with morning commuters. All manner of vessels follow slowly (barges, scows, skiffs, and tenders) bearing produce and supplies for the city.

We leave for our first excursion through the narrow entry that is the "street" whose location baffled us the evening before. The main route to the nearest square is a passageway that is barely six feet across and crowded with hurrying Venetians on their way to work. A few citizens stroll with their dogs and stop to talk with neighbors and shopkeepers who are busy opening their shops.

(* see page 132)

Following the signs to San Marco Square we emerge into the brilliant sunshine that illuminates the Piazza San Marco. There are puddles of water from the high tide that has overflowed into the square, and piled up around us are walking platforms that served as elevated walkways just a couple of days ago to keep visitors feet out of the water. As we step into the piazza, we are awed by the panorama.

To the left is the Basilica, a Byzantine structure with multiple rounded domes and gilded mosaics arching over each portal. Flanking the cathedral is the Doge Palace, whose walls are outlined by geometrical patterns sketched into a soft white and pink marble surface. Strolling through the crowd of fellow visitors and the always-present pigeons, we turn to see the expansive square.

It is the perfect picture of Venice we have carried in our mind's eye. Notwithstanding, now that we are here, we see the grime of the years layered on many surfaces. We note the endless cleaning projects and the clever trompe l'oeil digital photo that has replaced the facade of the clock tower while it is under construction. It fooled us as it will the many viewers of the thousands of photographs taken home by tourists.

In front of us is the Campanile, and at this very moment, gathering in front of the arched loggia at its base, are decorated officers of the Italian armed services and small platoons of men and women from the various divisions. They are in dress uniform, some with feathers in their hats, some with capes, and their commanders are covered in ribbons and gold and silver medals. It is a patriotic ceremony to recognize Italian military bravery from 1943 until the present. There is martial music and patriotic speeches in which we detect the names of Afghanistan, Iran, Bosnia, and Iraq clearly enunciated in the list of countries in which the military has served. The mayor, sporting a red, white, and green banner across his chest, inspects the troops and takes his place in the reviewing stand of dignitaries.

Though this scenic postcard in which we stand is not flawless, we recognize the length and depth of the history of this legendary city. The power of the city-state ruled by the doges, the waterway that opens into the ocean and unites the city with the world, and the very architecture of the buildings reflect the hundreds of years of existence and extensive worldly contact. In spite of the buildings that need cleaning, pesky pigeons underfoot, and tour groups stumbling over each other to capture perfect pictures, this city has endured from the era of the doges to the present. No longer an independent city-state, it remains a constant and assured presence in Italy and in Europe.

There are more places to explore, and we are off to search out the sights: the Accademia to view the paintings of Tintoretto, Titian, and Giorgione; the Rialto Bridge to look for gifts of earrings and beads and to browse the shops inspecting the handcrafted lace and masks; and the Jewish ghetto to visit a small museum in which the story of the Venetian Jews is told in photos and texts. We wander about and discover small cafes for ice cream and cappuccino and trattorias for our evening meals.

One day we take a ferry to the island of Murano and watch skilled artisans and their apprentices heat unformed glass in hot ovens and mold the fiery red mass into objects of art. There are so many kinds of glassware, chandeliers, vases, and art objects. Our senses are saturated and we are unable to make a decision as to what to buy. We take another ferry to another nearby island called Burano and are elated to find it to be so small. There is only one short street attractively lined with houses, each painted a different color. The shops are more manageable than in the big city, and we purchase a lacy tablecloth. We eat outdoors in a small restaurant and vary our daily pasta course to taste some of the local fresh fish catches.

A few days later, at the end of our visit, we reverse our steps and take the vaporetto to the bus station. Our brief respite from traffic congestion comes to an end when a police boat passes with blue lights flashing. All canal traffic comes to a standstill. Waiting with the crowds at the vaporetto stop, we are astonished to see an enormous construction barge topped by a derrick pass by going downstream. "It's from the construction site at the train station where they are building a fourth bridge over the Grand Canal," explains a local fellow passenger with a resigned glance. We grasp his message and prepare to wait with the calm and serenity that we are just beginning to understand during our short Venetian visit.

November 2003

A view of the Grand Canal
Venice, Italy

***About Venice**

***Venice,** the city known affectionately as "La Serenissima," was founded in the 9th century and is built on 117 islands, linked by 150 canals and 400 bridges.*

***St. Mark's** body is buried in the Basilica.*

***"Doge"** was the title of Venetian rulers and originates from the Latin word **dux** - leader.*

*The **Campanile** is a medieval bell tower, destroyed by fire and rebuilt in 1902.*

*The **Accademia** is the largest art museum in the city and is filled with original paintings of numerous Renaissance masters.*

*The **vaporetti** (singular – **vaporetto**) are public transport, water taxis, which can be privately hired, as can gondolas for scenic (and rather expensive) tours.*

***Murano** is a nearby island known for handmade glass factories and shops with showcases.*

*The island called **Burano** is famous for the lace woven there and the multicolored facades of the houses.*

Las Vegas – Inside and Out

Hot, dry, brown sand and brush. The desert lies outside of the neatly pruned and watered gardens of the town. The boundary is abrupt except for where underground springs, that inspired the early Spanish explorers to call the valley "The Meadows," reveal their telltale moisture in the greenery of scrub plants that struggle to survive. The air is dry; the heat is nevertheless debilitating. Only the bravest venture out in the more than 100-degree heat. Mostly the landscape is left to the snakes, sagebrush, and tumbleweed.

Silver, gold, saloons, and legalized gambling. Powerful motives for the first hardy trekkers who entered the valley, settled, and became residents. Caravan paths became railroad routes. The population grew and the ranches were transformed into desert retreats. Obliging laws made divorces quick and marriages easy. In 1940, Bugsy Siegel opened a club he named The Flamingo. Highway 91 became known as "The Strip." In the 60's, Howard Hughes enticed big entertainers from Hollywood and huge numbers of their fans followed.

Dim, cool, seemingly airless. There are no clocks, no windows, no open floor space between the banks of slot machines and gaming tables. Night and day do not exist. The machines and tables are continually illuminated. The intense evening crowds, the casual daytime player, and the few careless midnight players are all intent on one activity: betting their money against the house. Waitresses in brief skirts serve them free drinks. Uniformed attendants change bills to coins, answer questions, and direct the gamblers to the cashier. Silent cameras, in protected bubbles in the ceiling, stare at each gaming table.

A hotel that looks like the New York skyline, others appear to be the main square in Venice, a castle, a pirate ship, a space needle, and a pyramid. Each has fantasy attractions to draw the visitor inside: lion cubs, white tigers, acrobatic dolphins, dancing fountains, exotic gardens, and fabulous shows. The entrance to all of them, even the restaurants, rest rooms, and shops, require passage through large, darkened rooms that are the gambling casinos.

Outside, the desert, not far from downtown, remains as it always has. But today, the early oasis, situated over nourishing springs that once offered the simple comforts of food, water, shelter, and companionship, has become an indoor retreat dedicated to entertainment and illusion.

September 2001

Cafe Reinhard

The Ku'dam is quiet. A few cars pass by, and a couple, out strolling in the early evening, walk past the windows of the high fashion stores, stop at the intersection, and while waiting patiently for the light to change, consider eating at the cafe across the street. They can see the artwork that lines the walls above the heads of the well-dressed patrons. The diners chatter as they toast each other with raised wine glasses and sample their choices from the gourmet menu. As the couple enters, American swing classics from the 40's can be heard playing softly in the background. They are escorted to their table and relax in the elegant atmosphere.

A shadowy thought intrudes, slowly taking shape like a black and white photo. It is an image of this site 60 years ago, of rubble and wreckage. Tanks roll in the streets. Soldiers hide and fight among the ruins. Down the block, the steeple of the Kaiser Wilhelm Church is bombed out and resembles a hollow tooth. The Unter den Linden is stripped of its lovely linden trees and the avenue widened so military parades can pass by. The soldiers march in goose steps and create an unforgettable profile. The Reichstag is in ruins. The dome is missing. Left is a sunken space in the center of the destroyed building. Books are burned in the center square of Humboldt University. The building that was the headquarters of the SS becomes a pile of fragmented stones. The images don't stop. Forty years ago, a wall, fortified and unforgiving, is built to divide the east part of the city from the west.

Earlier in the day, the couple roamed about the city. Some things still remain to remind visitors and Berliners alike of a sorrowful past. The broken church tower stands silently gaping at the sky. A clear window in the center of the university plaza calls visitors to view a room below the ground, lined with empty, white bookshelves, a small, sad memorial to the book burning. At Checkpoint Charlie, the soulful eyes of an American soldier and a Russian soldier, captured in photographic portraits, stare down at today's visitors. A museum chronicles the wall's history, clever escape plans, and the impact it had on the city's inhabitants. A portion of the wall has been left standing a block away, holes punched in it by triumphant citizens who helped to knock down other portions. Poignant memorials to those who died trying to cross it are not far away.

Whether riding the bus, emerging from the underground transit, or walking around the city, today's visitors see new construction everywhere. Inside the reconstructed glass dome of the Reichstag, a ramp slowly winds around the inside and offers a wide-angle view of the city skyline. Seen below are the blue seats and the dais of the current parliament that once again governs Germany. The horses atop the nearby Brandenburg Gate prance in the air watching the cranes that renovate the city.

Tomorrow the couple will return to this lovely cafe to have coffee and watch the activity on the great avenue: a red Ferrari casually parked along the curb, late model cars crowding the pavement that forms the median strip, well-dressed citizens strolling by walking their dogs, and shoppers on their way to one of the largest department stores in Europe. On this day, in early spring 2002, in a city that strives to restore within itself the glamour and sophistication of earlier in the century, the heartbreaks of a painful past become shadows and are almost forgotten.

April 2002

Serendipity

St. Peter's Basilica, the Eiffel Tower, the Hermitage, the Kremlin. We have seen them all and more. The great wall of China, Michelangelo's David, the Opera House in Sydney. Testaments to mankind's ability to create magnificent art and architecture. Yet, in our travels we sometimes stumble onto commemorative sites that make us scratch our heads and wonder at what we are viewing.

In Stockholm, our short boat tour took us to one of the numerous islands that make up the city and into a ship museum. This special museum had one large vessel inside, preserved from the 15th century. Crafted entirely of wood, its tall masts, graceful bow, intricate masthead, and long sloping hull lined with gun ports for its many cannons made it an awesome example of craftsmanship and ingenuity. However, we learned that this impressive ship sank the first time it left port!

The story, as told in this museum of naval history, relates that this aggressive warship, pride of the Swedish Navy, carried a large number of heavy guns and could put forth tremendous firepower. To balance the weight of the guns and cannonballs, a ballast of rocks was stashed below the lowest deck. As the ship left port on its maiden voyage, the motion of the waves set up a rocking motion, and the ballast, proving itself to be insufficient, shifted to one side and the ship rolled over. We asked ourselves, are we looking at a monument to the clever, sea faring nation of Sweden?

While strolling in the streets of the beautiful city of Taormina, Sicily we found a small park filled with flowers and in the center was a monument that seemed to feature a small torpedo. We stopped to read the inscription and found that the site was dedicated to heroic Sicilian navy men from World War II.

What did these men do? They strapped themselves to a torpedo like the one on display and aimed themselves towards large enemy ships. Yes, they were kamikaze-like attacks, but the supposition was that the seamen would jump off just before making contact with their target. Hope so!

We were delighted to discover that Berlin is a city that has sprung back to life in the last 10 years. The painful past seems almost forgotten except for an occasional building purposefully left as a reminder. One day, as we were walking on the Kurfurstendamm, approaching the Europa Center, we noticed a sign that looked like the marker for a nuclear safety zone that we remembered from the 60's. Curious, we persisted in our investigation and found that, under a large building and filling an entire block, that there is a nuclear bomb shelter that remains intact underground. And, for a small fee, we could take a tour of it.

We climbed down about three flights of stairs and saw suspended in the darkness, beds that were little more than hammocks, hanging in tiers of three to accommodate up to 3000 people. We viewed separate latrines and showers for men and women, first aid rooms, control rooms, a breathing system that sounded like an iron lung, and rooms for food storage. In case of nuclear attack, the lucky people who were allowed in could wait out the horror...and, if not cooked in this confined, underground space, could emerge into the pulverized city and breath in the dust-laden radioactive air. Well, they had survived! Really!

May 2002

Scottish Fling

Glens and lochs, bagpipes, and kilts, Braveheart and Mary Queen of Scots. It is a country of varied legends and fantasies. Shakespeare captured the stories of King Malcolm and his grandson Duncan, and Hollywood has embellished the tales surrounding William Wallace and Robert the Bruce, crafting the saga of Braveheart. Mary Queen of the Scots, born in Linlithgow, united Scotland and England years before the official Act of Union.

The lore of Scotland beckons a visitor with capricious delights. What do they wear under those kilts? Is there really a fierce water-beast in Loch Ness? There are impressive historical remains – ceremonial circles and monumental tombs dating to the dawn of civilization – and a native language, Scottish Gaelic, trapped in time.

We have visited England many times, but never have we flown an hour north to explore Scotland until this year. The days are already quite long in April, and always, there is the rain. It is the lingering sun and hovering rain that create the mists that cast the old castles and forts into hazy and mysterious shapes. This country, whose borders extend to the North Sea, is filled with leafy glens and spring flowers on the hillside. Later in the year, we were told by our guide who rolled his "r's" and spoke with a wee lilt, the hills and valleys will fill with the multicolored heather now lying dormant in early spring.

On the river Clyde, the buildings of Glasgow, once dependent on industry, are dark and shadowy. We came to understand that the dusky buildings are made of the local soft sandstone and cleaning them seems to wash them away. The new buildings are bright and clean and will stay that way, because the city has taken care to prevent future pollution. The art galleries, concert halls, and museums that fill this city show the renaissance that the Glaswegians have planned to counter their commercial past.

The skyline of Edinburgh is made for photographers. As our tour bus lingers below the old city, we gaze upward, cameras clicking away, while we are told of the millennia-old volcanic cap and mile-long glacial slide that forms the rock on which is perched the Castle of Edinburgh, the Royal Mile, and the Queen's castle, Holyrood. Misty in the morning, sharply profiled with the towers of churches and castles in midday, and glimmering in nighttime illumination, it is a unique panorama. Cleverly the "old town" is the center of the summertime avant-guard Edinburgh International Arts Festival.

A daytrip to the countryside takes us north to the highlands known as the Trossachs and to the hillside dominated by Stirling Castle, site of a battle to separate the Scots from the English. Not far away are the "bonnie banks" of Loch Lomond, a deep, glacially cold and silvery lake. In the evening, in search of bagpipers and dancing, we book ourselves into a Scottish festival show. As expected, we are urged to eat haggis, assured that the traditional rough ingredients have been softened for the tourists. A kilted bagpiper accompanies slim young girls in twirling skirts dancing a highland fling and a sharp-footed male dancer who skillfully steps between the sharp swords lying beneath his flying feet.

On the flight back to London, we contemplate our short venture into a country that, though often overshadowed by England, nevertheless commands impressive attention for the numerous famous Scotsmen and women it has given the world: Mary Queen of Scots, Adam Smith, James Barrie, Robert Louis Stevenson, Lord Nelson, Davy Crockett, Alexander Graham Bell, Andrew Carnegie, Sean Connery...the list is long. Legendary and fabled, Scotland is now for us a destination full of intriguing memories to be savored and revisited.

May 2003

Sunset

The very edge of the old town faces due west, and each evening the crowds gather in the square to watch the sun settle into the horizon. There is a sunset somewhere every day, sometimes spectacular, sometimes just another ending to the day. But on this little spit of land in the Caribbean, there is something compelling about this daily event, known to the locals as the Sunset Festival, that makes the approaching darkness seem extraordinary. Ernest Hemingway and James Audubon came to witness it. Harry Truman, visiting from the capital, put aside his presidential duties to watch the daily phenomenon.

We are here to celebrate the beginning of the New Year. As we anticipate the exact moment the sun will disappear below the horizon, we are willing to follow the urging of the performers in the square to clap wildly to attract others to their show. They await our attention, momentarily focused on the horizon, to entertain us with a trained potbellied pig and cats and dogs that jump through hoops. One man has coached a pelican to submit to pats on the head. Another chains himself inside a straight jacket while upside down and brags that he will escape in four minutes.

It is 5:46 PM on this January afternoon. Through a few clouds, behind the full sails of the small boats positioned just beyond the square, the sun defies our attempt to look directly at its descent, flashes a solar goodbye, and is gone. The dusk deepens, and we wander off to look over the vendors' displays of jewelry, watercolor sketches (of sunsets, of course), T-shirts, natural sponges, and wind chimes. The sensual beat of a Latin combo draws us into a Cuban restaurant. Remembering that we are barely 90 miles away from that island we indulge ourselves and order *lechón asado* and *moros*.

The darkness is complete, though enhanced by Christmas lights still shining on the facades of the shops. We return to our hotel that faces a softly curved shoreline and think of tomorrow. From our balcony we will try to view the sunrise that starts the day, but if we miss it, we will be drawn at day's end to the tip of this western key to await another sunset.

January 2001

Sunset
Key West, Florida

Eulogy

Barney

1981 - 1992

It was silent, invisible, but ever present. Barney couldn't feel it and had no knowledge of its malignant presence. The operations to remove it were but small episodes in a life that was full of friendly people, comfortable sleeping spots, and fun with the family. But it took his life. It was a peaceful summer day and he slept as always, with his head on his paws. Then his breathing stopped.

We spoke to him softly for many days and went to his favorite places to be near him. We heard his barking when we returned home and were startled not to find him at the top of the steps. All of his friends – canine, feline, and human – inquired about him and were saddened to hear of his death.

Slowly we stopped speaking about him so our feelings could stabilize and our understanding friends would not be stretched to their limits. But we haven't forgotten him. He never spoke a word, and yet we felt his presence, his tolerance, his sensitivity to our moods, and his perpetual goodwill. We are surprised each time the seasons change and we are newly reminded of how our lives were intertwined.

Barney could not tolerate the heat, and we got used to inviting him to have a drink from the tub every time he returned from an outside break. He seemed to think the grand piano was a tree that would provide shade and would sleep under it until the sun went down. On cooler days or at sunset, he would sit high on our hill and survey the world.

Fall would find him asleep on the lawn amidst the leaves. Squirrels were fair game, but he and they knew he would never catch them. His huge size made him a lovable hulk that only human intruders would take seriously. As the weather cooled, we would find him sleeping in the freezing rain, seeming to enjoy the gray and frozen scene that surrounded him.

Barney loved snowstorms and would race around and scoop up mouthfuls of snow. He looked so silly as he enjoyed its cooling melt in his mouth. Cleaning the steps was a frenzied game for him as he fought the snow shovel in a contest of power. His hilltop was a favorite spot in the snow. He could watch the drivers negotiate the slippery streets in front and bark at the sledders behind him.

It was much too quiet this Christmas. None of the ornaments on our tree suffered from Barney's attentions. He would unerringly pick the ones that resembled animals or fruit. He didn't care to eat them; he just rearranged their shapes and left them to recover on the lawn outside. Our colored wrappings sat undisturbed because there was no Barney to shuffle through them, munching on the paper and tangling himself in the ribbon.

How will spring be? The perfumed evenings will be incomplete because his silent shape, sitting, sleeping, and waiting for us to come and sit next to him will be missing. The earth will renew itself but with one less creature. His absence will be noted by us, maybe silently, maybe with a glance or a whispered greeting. We will be sad but enriched because Barney was a part of our life.

January 1993

Smokey

You were not smoke, but rather shadow.
You hid and hunted in the dark,
pausing briefly, in the morning,
to linger on the front steps...
before disappearing for the day.

When no one watched,
you fled to your old home.
They brought you back and,
after a second good-bye,
you agreed to stay...for a while.

You've gone home again now...
They found your body
lying quietly under a tree,
your old hunting ground.
But your memory lingers
in our minds and hearts.

Sleep peacefully, Smokey,
your feline shadow now gone.

Smokey lived for 12 years
with our neighbors across the street

November 2000

My Cousin Vita

I didn't come to see you at the end and I feel that I neglected you. I couldn't bear to see you so sick that you were barely able to laugh – because that is what we always did together.

We never picked an appropriate moment. Usually those around us were crying and wailing over the death of some relative. But you and I...we danced and laughed and played games through all the solemn events. The worst part was when we were supposed to view the body. Neither of us wanted to do it and I don't think anybody ever persuaded us that it was the right thing to do. But now, you are the one who is to be viewed. Tell me, my cuz', now with whom am I to laugh?

I sent you beautiful roses...but I wanted to send you something more dramatic. I thought of a marijuana plant or an acacia, the African kind with thorns. No, my thought was not that you would have wanted such plants. It was the fun you would have had watching, from whatever venue, the expressions on their faces as your friends and your husbands (count all three of them) got an unexpected reaction from the homage they paid to you. Cool, Cuz'... I might have come out for that scene.

I look at us, those two young girls in the photo I sent you, and remember. You were the poised, confident one and I, the timid follower. You envied my settled family life, but I wanted to be like you, my city cousin whose life seemed exotic and exciting. We saw each other infrequently, but how we bonded when we did. I miss you, my cousin Vita.

I am laughing for the world to see when I relate the memories and scenes I've spoken of, but I am crying inside because I have lost my favorite cousin. I know, I know, you hate the tears. So it is up to me now to keep thinking about the funny things that made us laugh. My mind wanders back to those carefree moments we spent together and jumps forward to the out-of-control llama farm of your last years. I smile and dry my tears. It is with these memories that I want to remember you.

My cousin Vita died early in May 1998.
She was 63 years old.

May 1998

Goodbye Dad

My dad was a big man physically but his personality loomed even larger. He wanted to have his own way and could speak sharply and bluster his way into getting his demands satisfied. His determination scared me, but it was all that was needed to get me to do what he expected of me. Aloof from his grandchildren, he apologized for not knowing how to act around small children and regretted not knowing how to do the little things for them, like buying ice cream cones or bouncing them on his knees.

My father was a rich and complex character. He was a man who bridged continents and cultures. Even in this jet age, it is hard to fathom the strength needed to move from an Indian culture to an American one. He was the first son in a highly educated, high cast family. He was indulged and pampered, though often ignored by his intellectual father. He was Hindu and a vegetarian.

He came to America and never looked back at what he had left (though he never really learned to eat meat). He married an Italian in the days when Italians were subject to prejudice. And he found that he had married a woman who was equally strong and demanding. The two kept each other in balance.

He gave to my brother and me the awareness of the world around us. He and my mom hosted parties for their friends from around the world. He loved to talk philosophically with these friends and brought a broad and liberal perspective from his early education in India.

He preferred the elegant side of world cultures and found a way to help developing cultures as a UN expert. My mom had the travel bug, and he and she saw the world together. After her death, he retraced his trips with her to remember her and to keep his own horizons broad.

The month before his death he was planning a trip to Mardi Gras in New Orleans with a friend from Palm Beach. He knew he couldn't go, but he always said, "it is better to plan and not do it, than not to plan at all."

His friend and "angel" who cared for him at the end of his life will tell you that, though his final moments were peaceful, he began his last journey grumbling and protesting vigorously in the various hospital rooms to which he was sent. She never had a moment's doubt as to his demands and desires. He got his way to the end never succumbing to well-meant therapy, lousy hospital food, nor nurses who jostled and pricked him.

He is somewhere now searching for my mother from whom death separated him 12 years ago. He will move heaven and earth and will find her. Wherever he is, that place is rockin' to his demands. Heaven help them and him!

Madhu S. Gokhale was 91 years old at his death.
October 26, 1903 - December 5, 1994

December 1994

An egret
Tampa Florida

Adrienne Gokhale Cannon lives in Alexandria with her husband, Joel Robert Cannon, and their very large dog, Bear. She has three grown children and one grandson. Her son lives in Cambridge, England, with his family; her two daughters and their families live nearby in the Virginia suburbs.

Adrienne taught Spanish and Italian for 30 years in local high schools and retired from the Prince George's County, Maryland Public School System in 1996. Since that time she has been writing essays, playing the clarinet with community concert bands and volunteering as a tour guide at the Kennedy Center, Washington, DC.